THE WENDY WILLIAMS EXPERIENCE

ALSO BY WENDY WILLIAMS

Wendy's Got the Heat

THE WENDY WILLIAMS EXPERIENCE

WENDY WILLIAMS

with Karen Hunter

DUTTON

DUTTON
Published by Penguin Group (USA) Inc.
375 Hudson Street, New York, New York 10014, U.S.A.
Penguin Group (Canada), 10 Alcorn Avenue, Toronto, Ontario, Canada M4V 3B2
(a division of Pearson Penguin Canada Inc.); Penguin Books Ltd, 80 Strand, London
WC2R 0RL, England; Penguin Ireland, 25 St Stephen's Green, Dublin 2, Ireland
(a division of Penguin Books Ltd); Penguin Group (Australia), 250 Camberwell Road,
Camberwell, Victoria 3124, Australia (a division of Pearson Australia Group Pty Ltd);
Penguin Books India Pvt Ltd, 11 Community Centre, Panchsheel Park, New Delhi - 110
017, India; Penguin Group (NZ), Cnr Airborne and Rosedale Roads, Albany, Auckland,
New Zealand (a division of Pearson New Zealand Ltd); Penguin Books (South Africa)
(Pty) Ltd, 24 Sturdee Avenue, Rosebank, Johannesburg 2196, South Africa

Penguin Books Ltd, Registered Offices: 80 Strand, London WC2R 0RL, England

Published by Dutton, a member of Penguin Group (USA) Inc.

First printing, September 2004
10   9   8   7   6   5   4   3   2   1

 REGISTERED TRADEMARK—MARCA REGISTRADA

LIBRARY OF CONGRESS CATALOGING-IN-PUBLICATION DATA
Williams, Wendy.
    The Wendy Williams experience / by Wendy Williams, with Karen Hunter.
       p. cm.
    ISBN 0-525-94837-6 (hardcover : alk. paper)
    1. Celebrities—United States—Interviews.   I. Hunter, Karen.   II. Wendy Williams
experience (Radio program)   III. Title.
    PN1991.77.W46A3 2004
    791.44'72—dc22   2004010665

Printed in the United States of America
Set in Esprit Book

I dedicate this book to my husband and son, who give me the courage to get on the radio every day with fire on my tongue and no fear in my heart. I also dedicate this book to my mother and father, who have always encouraged my freedom of expression.

And lastly, but certainly not least, I dedicate this book to my fans—through love and hate, laughter and tears, I love you for listening!

Contents

CONTENTS

THE
WENDY WILLIAMS
EXPERIENCE

INTRODUCTION

The *Experience*

The *Wendy Williams Experience.* That is the name of my nationally syndicated radio show. But the *Experience* is almost twenty years of growth and insight. It is a reflection of where we have come from as a society and a reflection, in many ways, of where we are going. I started in radio at a crucial time in our history. America was going through the Reagan years of the 1980s, heading into a very selfish, me-first period. The thing that was called rap was evolving into a hip-hop movement. The thing called cocaine had moved into the darker period of crack and was infecting our neighborhoods throughout the country.

What was once fun and games was becoming very serious— in music and in life. And my career has chronicled this period. And as I have grown up, my radio show has become one of the history makers of our times. Some will say that perhaps I reflect the worst of what we human beings have to offer. I say, I reflect exactly what is out there in its natural state. If you don't like it, look in the mirror.

The *Experience* has evolved itself over the last decade into a brand of entertainment that I must say is totally *for* the people.

Many tune in to my show and think it's all about the gossip and all of that. But the show is, more than anything else, about you people and what you want to know about and what you have to say about the things going on. And as I comment on the things you want to know and want to hear, and relate these events to my own life, this show has become *the* experience.

Take, for example, my interview with Whitney Houston. Diane Sawyer had made history just a couple of weeks prior to my interview with Whitney. It was the second-highest-rated broadcast in entertainment history—behind Barbara Walters's Monica Lewinsky interview. A huge buzz followed Diane Sawyer's sit-down with Whitney. There was so much fodder for conversation that by the time I interviewed Whitney—who will be covered in great detail in a chapter in this book—people were still talking about it.

Diane Sawyer asked all of the right questions. In fact, for me that interview solidified Diane Sawyer's place as the number-one interviewer in the game. But . . . Diane Sawyer couldn't duplicate what I did with Whitney on the *Experience.* My interview with Whitney Houston was more than a one-on-one—it was a culmination of years of discussion on my show about her with the people. It was answers to the questions many of you had. And it was an insider's look into what was really the deal with Whitney. See, Whitney, for those listening to the *Experience,* is family. Her appearance on my show was like a homecoming long overdue.

While she was trying to keep it together in front of Diane Sawyer, on the *Experience* Whitney Houston could—and did—let her hair down. She could be herself. She was raw and got down and dirty—as you will see in the transcript of that interview.

And it was the best radio I had ever done. That interview was a prime example of what the *Experience* is all about. It's real. It's raw. It's about and for the people. And more than anything, it's not predictable. I love doing my show because it's as much a surprise for me most days as it is for you all.

And while I may go down in history as delivering the most interesting interview with one of our icons—Whitney Houston—my entire career has been built on such moments. I have become known for my celebrity interviews. People enjoy the kinds of questions I ask, they enjoy the kinds of answers I often provoke celebrities to give.

I don't do interviews based on a celebrity bio. People come into the studio with their publicist, a bio, and a list of questions I should ask. Pu-lease! That all goes in the garbage. I hate that. The last thing I get around to talking about when I do an interview is a celebrity's actual product of the moment. Boring! It might be that a person is coming out with a movie or a new CD. But we won't talk about that. I will mention it in the beginning and I will mention it in the end, but everything that goes on in the middle is about their personal lives.

I like to find out about people for the first time while the mics are open. If I have never met them before, I will learn about them when everyone else does. I don't want anything to taint the purity of the interview. During commercial breaks I won't even sit in the studio with my guest because I don't want to be tempted to have any conversation with them that might be interesting and then have to try and re-create that moment on the air. So in order not to waste one drop of entertainment, I will send my guest into the other room with their publicist or whoever they came to the studio with. And I will bring them back when the break is over. That formula has worked well for me over the years.

There are many celebrities, including rappers, and other entertainers who avoid my show like the plague. And there are others who are forbidden—by their handlers—from coming on my show. Babs from Da Band, which was featured on MTV's *Making the Band,* wanted to come up to the show to get some things off her chest. When her label, Bad Boy, found out, however, they put the clamps down and forbade her to come. That happens a lot. (She has since come on the show.)

But those with the courage to come on the show soon realize it's probably the best thing they could have done for themselves and their career. It's *not* coming on the *Experience* that can be detrimental to a career, because not only do we go on talking about those people anyway, but they never get to clear the air about such things as might be said about them.

Even those who I have had a sticky relationship with find that, in the end, the ordeal is not that bad. Once you get in the studio with me, it's a different story from what you might have expected.

I feel like I'm a very nice person (no, really!) and I try to be fair. I try to bring up as many things from the past that I've free-for-all talked about and I ask them if they're true. I dissect them as many ways as I can think of. *The Wendy Williams Experience* is the place where celebrities should want to come to clear up gossip, rumors, and innuendos. They have the opportunity to put their story out there. It's their chance to tell the people what the real deal is.

My show is almost a necessity if a celebrity expects to take it to the next level. Celebrities must share themselves with the public if they expect to stay on top. That's just the way it is today.

There are so many people out there with great talent. But what separates great talent from stardom is that surrounding excitement, that buzz. On the *Experience* I always use Deborah Cox as an example of someone who hasn't figured this out. Deborah Cox has a nice body; she's got a cute face; and she can really sing. So why isn't she as big as Ashanti or Beyoncé? I'm going to tell you why: She doesn't have a certain je ne sais quoi. She's boring. There are no rumors swirling about her. She isn't linked to anybody exciting. She's just another talented woman who will never be a superstar.

The National Basketball Association's Nets suffer from the same malady. Here is a basketball team that has beaten everyone in their conference and played for the NBA championship two years in a row. But despite their success, they couldn't seem to get sellout crowds in the Meadowlands. Why? Boring! You don't hear about any of those Nets out in the clubs, getting into trouble. You don't hear about them getting into fights or getting stopped by the cops for a DUI. None of them are linked to a sexy celebrity. They are just there—boring! Who cares?

Celebrities who put themselves out there—whether on purpose or by mistake—can really get some mileage out of their career. Look at Paris Hilton. She and her sister Nicky Hilton were mildly interesting. It was cool that these two rich girls would be on the red carpet and all of that, but it wasn't until Paris Hilton got caught out there with that sex tape that her career really took off. Because of the controversy, her television show, *The Simple Life,* became a hit. Now she is even talking about a music career, and that may fly, because people want to know Paris Hilton.

And there are those like Britney Spears who manufacture

buzz. Her kiss with Madonna (another pro in manufacturing buzz) was front-page news and a top story in entertainment for days. Britney was shown in the tabloids smoking, was reported to be a teen drinker, and even admitted to having used drugs. And I believe all of that has helped keep her at the top of pop. Her last album wasn't selling as well as the previous one, and what does she do? She gets a quickie marriage in Las Vegas. That marriage cost her more than half a million dollars in payoffs to the groom for an annulment, but how many more albums did she sell? Britney figured out that controversy sells. And it does.

So celebrities should be thanking me for keeping their names out there, because shows like mine help their careers.

I can't remember when I first started doing celebrity interviews the way I do them now. I cannot remember when I first started asking questions off the beaten path. But I can say that my style developed once I realized that I wanted to ask the questions and get the information for the *people,* not the industry. When I realized why I wanted to do radio, everything changed.

I do radio for the people, for John and Jane Q. Public. As a result I am not part of the "in crowd" of entertainment. I do not get invitations to some of the fabulous events and great parties that other disc jockeys, who are a little more kissy-kissy in their manner of interview, get to enjoy. But it's a sacrifice I gladly make.

Once I chose to be on the side of the people instead of on the side of the celebrity, I no longer had any boundaries in terms of the kinds of questions I could ask, because I was no longer worried about offending anybody. I wasn't worried about not being invited to their wedding or getting backstage passes to their concerts. It didn't take me long to figure out that I cared more about the people, my people, than about the celebrities.

LL Cool J was the very first celebrity I ever interviewed who is still a celebrity today. I was in college at Northeastern in Boston, and was a jock on my college station. We were actually one of the largest stations in the Boston area that played rap and R & B music. LL Cool J was just coming on the scene with "I Need a Beat," and was making his rounds promoting his new album.

He was about seventeen and I was . . . well, whatever. And I remember giggling and blushing through the whole interview. I don't even think I asked him one solid question; I was so caught up in his lip licking and his flirting. If he ever stopped flirting with me I would not have been ready to ask him any gripping questions, anyway. So the interview went much like this, "Ooh, LL, tell me about your new single," I said. "Well, sweetheart . . ." he began as he licked those lips of his about a dozen times. And I was finished.

The next time I interviewed LL Cool J was around 1995. He had become one of the biggest rappers in the game and had already broken into television with *In the House.* He had also done his first starring role in a movie in *Out of Sync.* I was the "it" girl at 98.7 KISS FM and was number one in my time slot, doing the popular Top 8 at 8 Countdown.

This interview was quite different. I wasn't falling for the flirtations. Somewhere along the way I realized that I wasn't somebody LL Cool J was checking for, or looking at in that way. I wasn't the "Around the Way Girl" he was rapping about. I was older and wasn't buying it. "Don't try to slay me with your lip licking," I was saying to myself. "I can see through it! You like small girls, not girls like me."

Let's just say, it was quite a different interview. He was seasoned. I was seasoned. He came in guarded and I was throwing questions that went way beyond "What's your next single off the album?"

Throughout the years, LL Cool J has been a topic of conversation on my show. Our talk about him prompted him to devote almost an entire chapter in his 1997 best-selling book, *I Make My Own Rules,* to discuss how I was such a negative influence and a terrible role model. To this day, if he sees me on the red carpet at a music award show, he will run in the opposite direction. And that's fine. We're not friends. But to me, he is still the GOAT— the greatest of all time—in rap music. That title, however, doesn't exempt him from being talked about on the *Experience.*

I have had the pleasure of interviewing so many icons and divas, so many stars and fading stars. And I have learned never to predict what is going to happen in an interview, because you never know. Even the most seasoned vets of the game can be thrown off course by an off-the-beaten-path question. I have had many interviews that I thought would be complete duds that turned out to be very exciting.

Judge Greg Mathis, of the *Judge Mathis* show, came on the *Experience* in 2003 for what I thought would be a perfectly boring interview about a man who pulled himself up from the streets and from a troubled past to become a judge and a role model. And it turned into a disgusting free-for-all where I was cussed out and yelled at. This judge completely lost his cool. I cannot give you any details about the question that I asked him that set him off. Unfortunately, after the interview Judge Mathis went back to Detroit and slapped a gag order on me, preventing me from ever talking about that interview or rebroadcasting it. But I can say this: It was one of my more memorable interviews that took a turn for the unexpected.

Voletta Wallace, the mother of the Notorious B.I.G, Christopher Wallace, was a guest on my show in the spring of 2003. She was coming on to promote "Big's Night Out," a charity event to raise money for the Christopher Wallace Foundation, which provides books and computers to schools primarily in the Brooklyn area where Biggie—who was shot to death in 1997— grew up.

I thought to myself, "This is going to be the most boring situation." In my mind I wasn't billing it as a full-fledged interview. Miss Wallace came to the show with R & B songstress Faith, who would normally get the *Experience* line of questioning—but because she was there as the dutiful daughter-in-law instead of as the First Lady of Bad Boy Records, I couldn't go there with her either. I mean, she was there with Miss Wallace—mature, motherly Miss Wallace. I couldn't ask those kinds of questions in front of her. Miss Wallace was bringing this dark cloud of maturity over the whole damn studio!

But I have to tell you, that woman just came in with her honesty, her smile, and her wisdomatic ways and changed everything I was feeling. She just lit up the room and ended up being one of my best interviews.

She was, surprisingly, a lot smaller in person. Her hair was done proper in an upsweep. Miss Wallace was not shiny. She was understated elegance. You could tell by the fabric that she was wearing good clothing, expensive clothing, but she wasn't wearing labels and jewelry. Miss Wallace was no Janice Combs, if you know what I mean.

And she was no wallflower either. Miss Wallace brought the heat. She not only talked about her age and how she hadn't had sex in *years,* but she also talked candidly about her son, Biggie, and his relationships with different women. The conversation led to Lil' Kim. And that's when it got interesting. There had been allegations made that Biggie was abusive to Kim during their relationship and that he even pointed a gun at her. Miss Wallace said, "If my son held a gun to her head, he should have pulled the trigger and blown her brains out!"

Whoa. She dropped that like a bomb and when the smoke cleared the entire studio was quiet. Hell, I imagined everyone in listening distance froze wherever they were with their mouths wide open. I mean, it was so quiet that you could hear a strand of hair from a weave hit the ground. And what was so crazy was that Miss Wallace meant every word. She was angry and she was dead serious. She was the Notorious M.O.M. That turned into one of my most memorable moments and it wasn't with a rapper or a singer or a movie star. It was with a sophisticated woman— a mother.

Another great radio moment was had with model Tyson Beckford. It was in 1999 while I was still in Philadelphia. I met Tyson for the first time in 1993 outside Club Bentley in New York. It was a hot summer night and he was with some of his boys. People knew Tyson Beckford back then but he wasn't a supermodel yet. He was just a model. I was better known in New York. We exchanged greetings then and it was all very pleasant.

I had never talked about Tyson on the air at this point. Oftentimes I find that if I've never talked about a celebrity but they know about my reputation, it is pretty easy to meet them. If I haven't talked about them, then there's no dirt on them. Or you can look at it that perhaps if I haven't talked about them that they need to heat it up a little. Because my radio show, for good or for bad, is reflective of what the people are talking about. And if you're a celebrity and I'm not talking about you, then you aren't at the top of your game.

Tyson certainly stepped up his game. Through the years, I got to learn more about him and he became fodder for the *Experience.* We would talk about Tyson and his bikes—he was into motorcycles. Tyson and his lady friends. Tyson and his guy buddies. We started teasing him on the radio. Tyson is a New Yorker and it's a small island and a lot of your business gets out. And then we started talking about Tyson and New York Yankees captain Derek Jeter.

The first time I got to interview Tyson on the radio was when I was in Philadelphia doing the morning show. He was scheduled to come on to talk about a major promotional event he was doing in town for Polo Ralph Lauren in conjunction with my station.

He got into Philly and apparently upon turning on the radio realized, "Uh-oh, Wendy is a part of this show!" See, the morning show in Philly was called the *Dream Team Morning Show.* My name wasn't in the title and Tyson had no idea I was there. When he got into the Philly area and heard it was going to be me who would be interviewing him, there must have been a panic in his camp. But it was too late to back out of the promotion because Polo and my radio station had sunk a lot of money into it. So his people called up my general manager at home and said, "Look, if she says anything out of order, he's leaving and not doing the promotion! Polo will never work with you again!"

Oh, it was a big stink. My general manager called my program director, who called me in the studio with a very stern voice and a very firm delivery talking about "You better not blow this for us!" He told me that I couldn't ask him questions centered on his relationships, his sexuality, his sexuality, and his sexuality. Well, I do have other lines of questioning, everybody!

So when he walked into the studio, he plopped down into the swivel chair and he swiveled around with his back to me, facing my two cohosts. My two partners knew what was going on and they found it to be the most comical thing, so they were ripping him. So he swivels away from them, too, and faces the wall during the entire interview. He conducts the interview facing the wall with sunglasses on. The whole interview became about Tyson and his anger toward me. It was very funny.

I ended up asking him about who he was dating and about his sexuality. I didn't ask in a way that would get me in trouble, though. I said, "Tyson, I already got the memo and I can't ask you about your sexuality and I can't ask you about your relationships. Why is that, Tyson?" So I am asking him within not asking him. He was very curt, very cold. He gave me one-word answers and grunts. I still laugh about that interview.

The next time I got to talk to him was on the red carpet at the VH1 Fashion Awards in 2003. I was there filming a segment of my show, *Wendy Williams Is on Fire,* for VH1. I'm among the throng of media and paparazzi and I call out to Tyson as he walks by. He sees it's me and instead of walking on—the way many celebrities who see me do—he stops and creates the following scene.

Since our last interview in Philly, I had made it back to New York on the radio, and every so often Tyson Beckford would be a topic of conversation on the *Experience.* The rumors were heating up with Tyson and Derek Jeter, and one major rumor had it that Tyson had a tattoo somewhere on his personage of a Yankees symbol with Jeter's number on it and the initials DJ under that.

The rumor apparently got back to Tyson, who, upon seeing me on the red carpet, started to disrobe right there. He took off his shirt while the paparazzi around us were looking like "Ooh, what is Tyson doing?!" No one knew what was going on, but they were loving it. We became the center of attention on the red carpet. Tyson made quite a spectacle as he pulled off his shirt and started gesticulating and carrying on. He turned around to show me his back. He turned and showed me his pecs and his arms. He turned his wrists inside out to show me that there was nothing there either. "See, nothing!" he said. "No 'DJ,' so stop it! Tyson Beckford is not gay, so stop it!"

It was moment of high drama. And it made for a great experience. I loved Tyson for that moment.

Most of the celebrities who I interview are amazingly candid and open. I believe they recognize the unique opportunity of coming on the *Experience*. A lot of people ask me why people don't just walk out when things get too hectic. Walking out is the absolute worst thing a celebrity can do. And in my almost twenty years doing radio I have only had one person actually walk out on me—Flava Flav from Public Enemy.

I was in Philly—where I actually had some of my wildest interviews. Oftentimes when a celebrity such as a rapper leaves New York to do media, they expect kid-glove treatment. They feel that perhaps other jocks in smaller markets aren't going to ask them the tough questions and that they can truly go on and promote whatever it is they want to promote.

But I brought my style with me to Philly. The easy interview time they thought they were going to have changed dramatically when they found out that I was part of that morning team on Power 99. "Oh, damn, I thought we got rid of her when she fell off the face of the earth after leaving New York," they would think. Wrong!

The interview with Flava Flav was quite crazy. He was very defensive. I asked him about his substance abuse, something he had been very open about in the past but wasn't in the mood to talk about on this day. Words were exchanged, and somewhere in there he called my mother a crackhead. I called him a bum and he ended up walking out of the studio. He went to the car in the parking lot, sulking. I didn't realize at the time that he was so pissed that he had to leave. I thought he had simply gone to the bathroom or something. I thought he was coming back. They managed to get him back into the studio after the show was over. He was still mad. Even when we took our promotional picture he was arguing with someone off camera about the whole thing.

But most people, even when they are feeling the heat, even if they want to leave, sit there and take it. They suffer through it and are better off for having done so. What I have learned through my years of interviewing and having people sweat through interviews—and almost everyone I interview, when it's over, has moist or sweaty palms, even seasoned vets—is that celebrities are basically cowards. And many of them do lots of the things that you hear me talk about on the radio.

Why not just stay and play it out? Even if they lie their way through it—and some have—it's better than making a scene or walking out. Staying and playing it out has proven to be your best weapon against *The Wendy Williams Experience.*

I have often thought about why more people haven't walked out or hung up on me, as I expected Whitney Houston to do long before she totally lost control of her senses. And I have concluded that they don't because they are afraid that it will never end, that I will continue to dig up bones on them. And they are probably right.

At the end of the day I do have the mic. And that mic is power.

CHAPTER
1
Scandality

Scandals, gossip, innuendos, rumors—we love it all! We love it because it takes us out of our own reality. It gives us an opportunity to look at somebody else's problems and know that we are not alone. Hell, if a celebrity is going through so much shit, our lives cannot be so bad after all.

There is another aspect to the world of scandal that we love too. Many of us love to hate. And we love to build people up to tear them down. We love to watch a celebrity take a fall. It reaffirms that even with all of their wealth and their fame and their success, they are just like us. They put their pants on the same way—one leg at a time.

I was introduced to the world of scandal at quite an early age. I remember being in the sixth grade and shopping in the Family Pharmacy at the Middlebrook Shopping Plaza, a little strip mall near my Ocean Township home. I was probably getting some candy or some other goodie to eat and while at the checkout counter, my eye caught a *National Enquirer* with its salacious headlines. I'm not sure what that particular one was about, but I remember buying it and reading it cover to cover. I was hooked.

I couldn't wait for the weekends or the summers, because that's when I could really get into the *Enquirer* and the *Star*. When I was growing up, most of the stories were about movie stars—stars of the big screen. There was always an item about Elizabeth Taylor and her relationships or her battles with drugs or something. There were stories about Farrah Fawcett and Ryan O'Neal, Diahann Carroll and Diana Ross, Natalie Wood, and even Jack La Lanne and Mike Douglas. And there was always something about one of the stars of *Dallas*. I loved reading every juicy morsel.

I also got hooked on *Divorce Court,* the original *Divorce Court*. And while I was young, and while what they were talking about was way over my head, I loved hearing the tawdry details of who was cheating on whom and why they were breaking up. I graduated to reading Dear Abby in the newspapers, which is probably where my desire to give advice was awakened.

So now, doing what I do in radio is about as natural as breathing. I didn't inherit this lust for the lascivious. My mother didn't buy the *Enquirer* or the *Star,* she wasn't into gossip. Neither was my sister, Wanda. That was my very own thing that I developed. And today someone is paying me for it!

Not a night goes by that I don't watch *E!, Access Hollywood,* and *Extra*. I must know what's going on. And I love working the red carpet. I want to know what the celebrities are wearing and what they are doing and who they are doing it with.

And oddly enough, I have become a leader in the gossip industry, someone whom the others call on when something goes down. They actually want *my* take on a particular scandal.

And for those who accuse me of creating this frenzy around gossip, I will tell them to look around—this thing has been going on long before Wendy Williams got ahold of it. That genie was let out of the bottle a while ago, and she's not going back.

Don't get me wrong, though. As much as I love the scandals, there is a part of me—the very human part of me—that is saddened by our lust for it. We have become desensitized to everything, and we seem not to care about people and their feelings or the impact that this stuff will have on our kids. We want to know and we want to know more. And it goes beyond celebrities. We even want to know what our neighbors and everyday average citizens are up to. That's why these reality shows have become so popular. It's sick, really.

The sickest things I have seen of late are images generated on these telephones that take pictures. I cannot tell you how many listeners want to show me a photo they took on the sneak from their telephone of someone doing something they shouldn't be caught doing. Those camera phones are the most evil invention. I wish they would go the fuck away. It's a great invasion of privacy.

So is the E! Celebrities Uncensored show, which spies on celebrities. Yeah, I watch it. But I do so with both hands over my eyes and my fingers separated so that I can barely see through them. I think shows like that go too far.

Am I a hypocrite for saying that? I guess you can call me a hypocrite. But I am still human and still a mother and understand the impact all of that has on society. Dammit! And damn us as a society for loving it so much. And damn me for sharing it and not being able to let it go.

There was a time when I was just a regular deejay, spinning the hits. But before I knew it, I had gone from spinning hits to telling people's business, and you people wanted to know more and more. It's to a point now where if I can get one song in during the course of an hour, I'm doing well. This gossip thing has had a snowball effect. The more I talk, the more people want. And believe it or not, I hate the *g*-word. I hate being identified as a gossip. It's ugly. I try to disguise it by saying we're talking about pop culture. But we all know what it really is.

I comfort myself by saying that gossip doesn't ruin people anymore. So many of us have dark pasts and secrets that we cannot afford to point our finger at the next person and judge. Thank God, we live in a forgiving society. And black people are among the most forgiving. So in terms of ruining someone, there are so many ways to make a wrong right. We don't have time to hold people's feet to the fire for but so long. Before we know it, there is the next scandal to focus on.

But there are a few scandals that I think we will be talking about for a while. The O. J. Simpson trial is something people still talk about, and it's been more than ten years since that verdict.

Did he murder his ex-wife Nicole Brown Simpson and her friend Ronald Goldman? What was that ride in the Bronco all about? And why didn't the glove fit? They still refer to his trial as the "Trial of the Century." Hell, it may be the trial of the millennium.

In 2003, I met O. J. Simpson—who, by the way, was acquitted of the double murder in the criminal trial but found responsible for the deaths in a civil trial—for the very first time on my radio show. My station, WBLS, which happens to be a black-owned radio station, set it up. They basically sprang the interview on me without asking if I even wanted to interview him (which I didn't).

Sometimes people feel that because we're all black, we all have to support one another. We all have to vote for the black man because he's running for president. We all have to believe the black man is innocent of murder because America shows black men so much injustice. Well, I'll tell you what, when they told me O. J. was at the station to be interviewed, I was upset. I was very upset. They never asked me if I wanted to sit face-to-face with someone who I believe is a murderer—someone who I believe got away with murder.

He was in town doing some sort of media something. Cameras were following O. J. around wherever he went, as he mentioned on my show, to document exactly how people treat him. He contended that people still love him and that only the media twisted his acceptance around:

Wendy Williams (WW): Interesting. So, um, when you travel and when you're walking down the street and things like that, what type of reaction do you get from people?

O. J. Simpson (OJ): The exact reaction may be a little more emotion—

WW: Okay.

OJ: —than I got fifteen years ago. If you took a walk with me down the street, you'd be amazed. I don't care where I go, white, black, wherever I go. Everybody's terrific; it's only the media that dogs me.

WW: I don't—

OJ: And that's one of the reasons why we're chronicling—

WW: I don't think so, O.J.

OJ: What do you mean, you don't think so? Hey, how many people [who] are in this room have been in various cities with me? You ask every one of them ...

(someone says something, claps)

WW: Really?

OJ: *You know what really bothers me?*

WW: *Okay.*

OJ: *Uh-huh. They were saying one thing and whenever I was asked I'd say everywhere I go people are terrific, right.*

WW: *Yeah?*

OJ: *Well, what happened was* Esquire *magazine—*

WW: *Uh-huh.*

OJ: *—decided to find out the truth.*

WW: *Okay.*

OJ: *So, I didn't know it, but for a month and a half they had a writer follow me.*

WW: *Okay.*

OJ: *And after a month they made themselves known to me.*

WW: *Uh-huh.*

OJ: *And they did a cover story, and what did the story say? No matter what anybody say, everywhere this guy goes, every-body, old ladies, young ladies—*

WW: *Really?*

OJ: *—white, black. Everybody's terrific wherever I go. I have trouble buying a drink in a restaurant. Last night I couldn't buy a drink when I got here at the hotel restaurant. People buy my dinner, they buy my lunch. And I mean, it's non-denominational, white, black, blue, green, it's whatever it is. It's the media and only the media [that tells a different story].*

He even talked about having a good relationship with the parents of Nicole Brown. He talked about himself and the Browns attending the school sports games of O. J.'s kids, Sydney and Justin. He said he is well received at those games too.

And I have to admit, he might be right. I found O. J. Simpson to be perfectly charming in person. He was actually very attractive to me. Yes, he charmed me. I still think O. J.'s a murderer, but he's a damned charming murderer.

First of all, he's sexy. O. J. Simpson is sexy. He has a full head of hair and he has the smoothest, most beautiful skin. And his body. You know, the man is older now and it's not to die for. But you can see what it used to look like and you can see it hasn't changed much. He has a nice physique. He's big and charming, with beautiful teeth and a nice smile. He came in, we talked about his relationships with white women. We talked about his image. We even talked about his relationships with black women:

WW: *When's the last time you had sex with a black woman, O.J.?*

OJ: *Well, a dark woman, she wasn't quite black 'cause she was Cuban, uh, it's none of your business, but that's the last one I've been with.*

WW: *But that's not a black woman, that was a Cuban woman.*

OJ: *Well, I like Cuban women.*

WW: *I'm talking about black like me.*

OJ: *Two years ago.*

WW: *Look at that. And in the meantime you've done a lot of boning between, uh, two years ago and now. And you skipped over the sisters.*

OJ: *Well, naw, naw, naw. I've done a lot of boning with two women. No more than two women. In that specific length of time.*

WW: *Listen, O.J.—*

OJ: *And I'm single.*

WW: *I know, but you have—*

OJ: *I can date who I wanna date.*

WW: *You have—*

OJ: *But I don't, it's . . . You're buying into this.*

WW: *No, well, O.J.—*

OJ: *You're buying into media. Everybody that knows me don't buy into it. The people that see me out don't buy into it. But you're somewhat, for some reason you're buying into the white media.*

WW: *O.J., have you ever dated women as dark as your charcoal pants?*

OJ: *In high school.*

WW: *In high school?*

OJ: *Now, I've dated numerous women that's about your color.*

WW: *And, look, I'm a nice little, as a matter of fact, we're the same complexion. I may be a little lighter than you and I am a real—*

OJ: *Is something wrong with us?*

WW: *I'm black as tar to you.*

OJ: *Nah, no, you're not. I told, I just told you I've dated . . . the girl that I dated, the last girl that we talked about I was with—*

WW: *Mm-hmm.*

OJ: *—was darker than you.*

WW: *But I bet you she had hair like [TLC's] Chili or [former MTV host] Ananda Lewis. Didn't she?*

OJ: *Thank God, she did!*

WW: *See, look at that. "Thank God, she did!"?*

OJ: *I like that hair. What's wrong with that? I gotta make excuses for what I like?*

WW: *No.*

OJ: (Chuckles.) *I like rocky road ice cream.*

WW: *You don't have to make any . . . That's one thing about this show—*

OJ: *But I still have vanilla ice cream from time to time.*

WW: *So, if a woman, um, so we'll go past that. You've already—*

OJ: *Yeah, just leave the women.*

WW: *Yeah, yeah, yeah. Cause the women right now are very, very mad. The women with—*

OJ: *I disagree with you—*

WW: *—our perms and our weaves and our—*

OJ: *—everywhere I go women are terrific. Wherever I go the women are terrific.*

WW: *The white women.*

OJ: *No, the black women. Wherever I go, women are terrific. Sisters have been the most supportive group of people to me than anybody in this country. I get more letters from them than anybody.*

WW: (Sighs.)

OJ: *Even kids who are sports fans.*

WW: *O. J.*

OJ: *Yes.*

WW: *I don't believe that, but we'll move on.*

O.J.:   *Okay.*

O. J. was very candid in his responses and he obviously wasn't trying to be politically correct. We got along very well. We drank champagne. He left.

And when he did leave, I thought, "Damn him! He's handsome. He's charming! He's a murderer."

I thought he was a murderer before I interviewed him. I

thought he was a murderer during our interview. And I still think he's a murderer. And he is still one of the most controversial figures of our time.

Michael Jackson is another. Actually, his scandals, both the 1993 child molestation allegations and the more recent one from 2003 (and the others that seem to be coming out the woodwork), might just define the legacy of Michael Jackson. And what a shame that would be. He has done so much for the world of music and is perhaps one of the most talented people ever to live, but he will be forever known as a man who is inappropriate with young boys—whether he is acquitted of the latest charges or not.

Michael Jackson, in my opinion, is guilty of something. I don't know what exactly, but he did something—even if it was only displaying very, very bad judgment. And it's just as much the fault of his father, Joe Jackson, for taking away his childhood as it is Michael's fault for being a grown man who can't seem to tear himself away from young boys.

And while it is easy to point a finger at Joe Jackson and the abuse he allegedly gave to Michael and whatever psychological problems he may have caused, I believe that at forty-five years old you are supposed to have gotten past whatever burdens your parents may have put on your shoulders. And if you haven't completely gotten over the things your parents did, at forty-five you should at least be able to manage those issues in an adult realm.

Don't get me wrong, parents can do stuff that will mess you up, that you will carry with you into adulthood. But at some point you still have to accept responsibility for the things you do, regardless of the root problem.

When I look at Michael Jackson, I'm not judging him based on some of the craziness he displays. And I believe people are looking at the wrong things when they look at his relationship with a young Emmanuel Lewis or a young Macaulay Culkin. Those weren't the smoking guns, so to speak. I don't think Michael would be guilty of anything with those kids—they're too high profile. But with the twelve-year-old boy dying from cancer? This is the boy who was featured in that Martin Bashir special with Michael Jackson—the same boy who claimed that Michael saved his life and helped him to overcome his cancer. Wasn't he supposed to die from that cancer? No victim, no witness. Hmm.

Again, this is about what I believe to be the biggest problem in our society—child molestation. Even if Michael Jackson did nothing sexual with that twelve-year-old boy, was it appropriate to have that child sleep over so many times? Perhaps he created an environment where that child crossed the line in his mind, not thinking that there was a line. And that to me is a crime. Adults need to make boundaries with children and make those boundaries very clear. Children must know their place and adults must make that place very secure and clear for them.

I don't know what happened in Michael's childhood, but I do know one thing about abuse—if it isn't dealt with or corrected, the cycle is never broken.

When the latest Michael Jackson scandal broke in 2003, I had the opportunity to actually talk with Michael's mother and father, Katherine and Joseph, on the radio. I have Steve Manning, celebrity publicist, to thank for that interview. Steve is very close to the Jackson family. He is so close that he spends Thanksgiving at the Jackson compound.

Through Steve, I was even invited to the Jacksons' to celebrate Joe's birthday in August of 2003. I didn't go because I didn't want to taint what I do—which, I have said, is not for the celebrities or to be in with them, but for the people. But we did talk on the air about the party I missed, and Katherine even asked me where I'd been. When my previous book, *Wendy's Got the Heat*, came out, Katherine and Jermaine Jackson requested a copy, which I signed and sent to them. I like the Jackson clan. But I have to call it like I see it. My liking for them cannot hold me back from saying what I feel about Michael and this situation. And I am disgusted by it.

I have no idea how this particular case is going to turn out, but I pray that if Michael once again walks, he walks himself somewhere to get some help, because he has some serious problems.

Unfortunately, Michael Jackson is not alone. The sex scandals of the 1980s, 1990s, and 2000s, coming from the one place we should never expect such scandals, helped shake many people's very faith. I'm talking about the scandal with Jim Bakker and the PTL Club, the sex scandal with Jimmy Swaggart, and the sex scandals that are still rocking the Catholic Church. Perhaps these scandals have done more damage than the allegations about Michael Jackson ever could, because as a result of these scandals people have turned away from their religion. I see a lot of people seeking answers and searching in different places, from studying the kabbalah to joining the Church of Scientology. The public can no longer depend on the people and the institutions that should be above such behavior. With celebrities we can sometimes expect the worst, but from the church? Wow!

Whitney Houston's admission of drug use in 2003 could potentially be a scandal for the time capsule. But I am hoping it doesn't happen. I am hoping she is in a passing phase—that she will clean herself up and become once again one of the reigning queens of our time. But if she does do a Billie Holiday, which she seems unfortunately headed toward, then hers will truly be a scandal for the ages. But we have to wait and see.

In 2003, squeaky-clean NBA star Kobe Bryant shocked the

sports world with his arrest for rape. Kobe Bryant—the fresh-faced, near-perfect, endorser's dream—arrested for rape. Surprised? Not me.

When I first heard about the Kobe Bryant scandal, I said immediately that he's probably guilty. Guilty of "taking it." *Rape* is such a harsh word, and I'm not sure that I would use the word for what I believe Kobe Bryant did. I think it's unfair to use the word *rape* about a woman who willingly went to a hotel room and who pretty much knew the score and through her own damn naïveté got tripped up into something she didn't want. I know because this happened to me.

When I think of rape I think of the woman in the alley whose clothes are ripped, whose face has been scarred, who has been brutalized. I don't like to use the word *rape* for what happened to the girl in the Kobe Bryant situation. I will call it nonconsensual sex. According to published reports, she agreed to some form of sex with him but didn't consent when he wanted to do something else with her. I believe she said no. And I also believe that when she said no, he took it. He should not have taken it. But she should not have put herself in that situation. And then there is the question about whether it was all a setup in the first place.

Men like Kobe Bryant are very susceptible to having things like this happen to them. Men who are wealthy, famous, star athletes, actors, wealthy businessmen, can all get got like this. It can happen to any man with money and a willing participant—a girl who is after a few dollars or some attention.

But what happened to Kobe Bryant is one hundred percent his fault. Ultimately, he's a married man and he got his just deserts because he was cheating on his wife. Cheating on his wife, without a condom, no less! Damn him! And now he not only has to deal with a trial and potential jail time, but also his wife, Vanessa, and her attitude toward him for cheating in such a disgustingly up-high way. I mean, there was nothing down-low or discreet about what Kobe did. And his wife, like so many other women in that position, also has got to learn about being an NBA player's wife and that this was the only time he got *caught.*

But even though the media—myself included—are guilty of making this a huge, huge story, Kobe Bryant's case is all too common. And I wonder how history will treat the Kobe Bryant scandal or the scandal involving former NBA player Jayson Williams, who killed a limo driver in his home, or the scandal of rocker Phil Spector, also accused of murder in 2003, or Robert Blake, who was accused of an O. J.-style killing of his wife. Will we even care? Will we be so bombarded with other scandals that we won't even remember these?

There is one scandal that I know I will never forget—the R. Kelly sex scandal. Unlike the rest, this one feels personal, because before the scandal R. Kelly was one of my favorite entertainers.

In the middle of the week I received an afternoon call. I had been back in New York perhaps a month at WBLS-FM and the *Experience* was reestablishing itself as *the* place to go if you wanted to know what was happening in the world—as far as celebrities are concerned. We were bringing the heat from the start.

The caller said that he had something that I *had* to see. He would meet me downstairs after the show. I got downstairs to see a black limousine and the person inside was a record-label executive—a high appointed record-label executive. If I mentioned his name, you would know who he is.

In the limo was another man, who had traveled all the way from Chicago to deliver the goods. My husband and manager,

Kevin, was there as well. The four of us huddled around a monitor in back of the limo as the executive popped in a VHS tape. What I saw to this day makes my stomach turn. I watched in utter disgust. But I also watched very carefully, taking in every detail, because I knew in my gut that I would never see this tape again—not because I wouldn't have access, but because what I saw was so repulsive that I knew I could not watch it a second time.

Everything had to register, because I knew I was going to get on the air the next day and tell exactly what I saw. And what I saw was a man who looked just like R. Kelly performing sex acts with females who looked just like little girls.

It appeared to be somewhere in R. Kelly's house. There were R. Kelly platinum plaques on the wall. I even saw an Aaliyah plaque on a wall in the background. The man who looked like R. Kelly was very aware of the camera. There were three sex sessions on this video with three different young ladies.

In the first session, the girl looked about sixteen years old. She could have been as old as twenty, because I admit that sometimes young girls look older and some older women look very young. The man was having sex with her in a chair. The second session was blurry. It was difficult to make out the girl's features, but it was clear that it was the same man and it was clear that the young lady was very young. But it was the last session that blew me away.

That is the one that anyone who has seen this tape will remember in vivid detail. There was a young lady—a very young lady—who looked to be between thirteen and fifteen years old. She had a little girl's body, not fully developed, barely any hair growing in certain areas.

The man was apparently sitting on a couch, holding the camera as the young lady danced—it was a hootchie, nasty, strip-club dance. Midway through the dance she spread her legs like an Alvin Ailey dancer and urinated. The man holding the camera directed her to do it. He was directing her the whole time, saying things like "Turn around now and touch yourself." It was very, very disgusting and disturbing.

The man with the camera, who looked like R. Kelly, then stepped into the frame and had the young lady spread out on the couch. He stood over her and urinated on her chest and watched as it ran down her body. I had seen enough. There was more on this tape, much more.

The record executive had gotten it from a man from Chicago, who happened to be someone in R. Kelly's camp. He was disgusted by what was happening and felt that the record executive could somehow put a stop to it. The record executive did one of the first things he thought of—brought the tape to me. He knew that I could put light on this tape the way no one else could. And I did. I broke the R. Kelly story on the air the next day.

It was emotional for me to tell this story on the air. Comedian/actor Bill Bellamy was my guest in the studio. He was there to promote his new series, *Fast Lane,* which was debuting on Fox (it has since been canceled). Bill is from New Jersey and we go way back—we are from the same generation and kind of started in the business together. Bill was there as I was telling this story, and at one point I became very emotional as I was describing what I had seen.

Yes, it was disgusting. But I was thinking about these young girls in the video. Our problem isn't the war on drugs and all of that—which is important—but the sexualization of our children is what is killing us as a society. Older men preying on the young boys and girls is a huge problem that no one talks about. This R. Kelly scandal just really hit home with how prevalent this is, and our community is just so forgiving.

I started to cry on the air. The tears that I was shedding were for the girls this is happening to—these girls whom I will defend to the end because they simply know no better. I was also crying because I knew that in spite of what I was saying on the air and in spite of what I had seen in that video, R. Kelly's fans would still buy his records, radio stations would still play his music, and he would still win awards.

At the 2003 BET Awards, R. Kelly not only performed but he won the Best Male R & B award. He was also nominated for a Soul Train Music Award and a Grammy in 2004! His album *Chocolate Factory,* released in March of 2003, sold more than 532,000 copies its first week, and by May of that year it had sold more than two million copies. In June of 2003, R. Kelly made the top of the R & B/Hip-Hop Single Sales Chart with his single "Snake." The next month the single crossed over onto the Top 40 list. In August of 2003, his next album, *R,* went eight times platinum—that's eight million copies sold. And the video for the song "Ignition" was nominated for an MTV Video Music Award. In September, R. Kelly was nominated for two American Music Awards. He was even nominated for a 2004 NAACP Image Award. An *image* award! Who says that crime doesn't pay?

I get a lot of criticism for telling people's business. I get a lot of flak for "gossiping" about celebrities on my show. Well, I will say this: If I don't tell it, who will? And I do what I do because I am tired of seeing these people—these celebrities who have the attention and the ear and eye of so many young people in our society—get away with the things they get away with.

Perhaps people will still buy their records, but maybe talking about them gives people a chance to examine a little more closely these people they have put on a pedestal.

By the way, at the time of this book's publication, R. Kelly was standing trial on charges of child pornography. He had been indicted on twenty-one counts of child pornography stemming from the sex on video, including the one that I saw with the girl who turned out to be thirteen years old.

This R. Kelly scandal hurts me particularly, not only because of the hurt unleashed on the young girls, but also because R. Kelly happened to be one of my favorite singers of all time. I'm not a concertgoer, and I never get excited when I hear people are going to be in concert, because I'm usually attending as part of my job. The only concert I have been to in recent years for fun was an R. Kelly concert in New York in 1997 or 1998. My husband and I sat near the stage and we danced in the aisle and the whole bit and had a great time.

The first time I met R. Kelly I was at 98.7 KISS in the early 1990s. He was part of a group, Public Announcement. He talked about how he was singing in the subways of Chicago for money. He talked about how close he was to his mother (who has since died). I remember thinking how country and corny he was back then and also how talented. And there is still something country and corny about him to me even to this day.

I have to tell you that the sexual scandal that happened with him has turned me off from listening to any R. Kelly music with the same fever—except for happy songs like "Step in the Name of Love," where I can insert my own person that I want to step to. I no longer think of music when I think of R. Kelly.

When I went to his concert and he was talking about bumping and grinding, before the scandal he was bumping and grinding for me. Now when I hear that song, I think, "Ilk!" because all I can see is him bumping and grinding with little girls and I'm thinking, when he pulls women up on the stage to perform in his show, "You don't—allegedly—even like women of that age." Yes, until he is convicted (or if he is convicted, because you all know that money talks), it is still only alleged. But I know what I saw in the video. I saw him doing unthinkable things to a little girl.

I still think about this case, and no matter how it turns out, in many ways it is an example of what I was saying earlier—we are a forgiving people. No matter what scandal celebrities find themselves in, ultimately, after we've finished raking them over the coals and talking about them, we will still love them. They are *our* celebrities.

CHAPTER

2

One Bad Dude

Suge Knight is by far the scariest figure in hip-hop. From his imposing size—about six feet four, three hundred and fifty pounds—to his even more imposing reputation, this man is the real deal. He is the ultimate regulator in the game.

Am I scared of him? No. Do I respect his gangsta? Do I have a choice? I mean, do any of us have a choice?

I interviewed him for the first time in the spring of 2003. He had just gotten out of prison after serving time for his first parole violation. He had to get permission from his parole officer to travel to New York for the interview, and permission was granted. This was my first face-to-face with the giant mogul, and I found him to be surprisingly honest and open.

I was also surprised to find that Suge Knight is quite a conversationalist. He might actually be one of my all-time favorite people to interview. Not only is he very honest but he is also very dramatic. When you ask him a question, he doesn't just answer. He goes through this whole dramatic ritual—he will pause, then take a long pull on his fifty-dollar cigar. He dims his eyes, sits back, and then blows out the smoke, long and smooth, into the air. If he likes the question, he will even crack a smile. All of this drama before he parts his lips to actually answer the question. I love that.

And I love that Suge's not afraid to smile. As tough as he is, he has real, honest emotions. Hell, he's just real honest, period. He even told me he was watching his weight when I questioned him about drinking a Diet Coke. Imagine that? I like the dude for that.

There is also a certain kind of justice with the way Suge conducts himself and his business. There is a code of ethics, so to speak, with him. It's weird, but he actually draws a line in the sand and has very high views when it comes to ethical issues like snitching and betraying a confidence and even allowing sex or relationships to get in the way of making money. Suge Knight lives by rules. He is very disciplined and serious when it comes to his business, and he doesn't like it when other people allow their weaknesses to get in the way of conducting proper business.

Suge, unlike most men, cannot be easily caught up in the punani.

Suge Knight (SK): You can shake your ass at me all night long.
Wendy Williams (WW): Okay.
SK: That don't mean I gotta touch it. (Laughs.)
WW: You know, somehow I believe that in you. Somehow I believe that your boys are doing a whole lot more boning than you.
SK: Definitely.
WW: Because you understand the asset of having a clear mind for business.
SK: Well, you know, my whole thing is that, you know, can't nobody get to a level that they need to be on.

WW: Mmm-hmm.

SK: See, this is your weakness. Drugs is a weakness.

WW: Yes.

SK: Okay, if you a drunk and you abuse alcohol, that's a weakness.

WW: Yes.

SK: A woman can be a weakness.

WW: Yes! Absolutely.

SK: Or, a man can be a weakness.

WW: True.

SK: 'Cause the thing is this, if I have an artist and she a woman and she in the studio . . .

WW: Mmm-hmm.

SK: And it was pagers then, now it's e-mails.

WW: Mmm-hmm, mmm-hmm.

SK: Two ways, they need to throw those shits out!

WW: I hate them.

SK: So if that can go off and her dude can e-mail her and tell her, "Who you up there messing with?" or accuse her of something, and it throws her whole session off, I have a problem with that.

WW: Yeah.

SK: She on my time. She on my money. We trying to create something.

WW: Have you ever—

SK: So, at the same time, that's the same thing with a guy. So back to what I was saying as far as I don't use drugs, and all that type of stuff. And if you abuse that, then how could you be on point? How could you be focused? How could you know what's going on?

WW: I hear that.

SK: *And if you always chasing women everywhere you go, how could you get what you need to do? Can't do that much shit, ain't that much time in the day.*

Too many in the game of hip-hop are sloppy when it comes to their business, and I respect Suge for keeping boundaries on his stuff. Yes, I definitely respect him.

Whenever Suge and I get together, it's all about business. It's not about the drinks and the parties and the laughing. Now, don't get me wrong, whenever my husband and I are in Los Angeles, Suge has been perfectly wonderful. Whenever we see him, we make sure we have all of the latest numbers and two-way contacts and all of that. He invites us places and he's told us that whenever we're in town, he's there for us for whatever we need. But we've never taken him up on his offer.

There are some people who, the more time you spend around them, the bigger hole you dig for yourself with them. And I don't want to be in too deep with Suge Knight. I want it to be business and when it's over, we can shake hands, hug, and part ways.

But it's genuine love between me and Suge. It's business love. Respect. And I want to keep it like that. You never know when a person like me will need a person like Suge. And you never know when a person like Suge will need a person like me to expose someone.

I like our relationship. And I like Suge. He represents the rags-to-riches of hip-hop. He started Death Row, which is now Tha Row, with just a thought and he built it into a formidable label. Suge represents the absolute struggle in this game and he proves that if you stay on the grind long enough, you will succeed.

Who is Suge Knight? His mother says he's a wonderful man

who never gave her a moment's trouble as a child growing up. He comes from what appears to be a pretty stable two-parent household. He didn't grow up poor. He is college educated.

WW: *Your mother and father are still together?*

SK: *Yeah. They been together since, like, my mother was fourteen.*

WW: *Wow!*

SK: *My father was probably like eighteen.*

WW: *Have you ever fought your father, physically?*

SK: *Nah, I never fought my father physically. I wouldn't fight my father, you know.*

WW: *You didn't grow up like that.*

SK: *I grew up with believing in respecting your parents. One thing I believe in, I believe kids is a blessing, respecting kids and old people. Now these grown people . . . so, but as far as kids and old people, I always got respect.*

And because I have such respect for Suge Knight, I don't cross the line with him. He might be the only person who, if there is something he doesn't want me to ask him about, I won't. I cannot think in my recent career when I have agreed to that. Perhaps when I first started out, before I was *the* Wendy Williams and was just some jock trying to make it, I would follow the lead of a celebrity. When I was first starting out, if an artist or celebrity said to me, "I don't want to talk about that DWI or my baby's mother," I would say okay. But in the last decade or so, that hasn't happened. I ask any and everything I think to ask, and I never care what *they* want me to ask or not ask. You come on the *Experience,* and all bets are off.

But Suge asked me not to talk about his women. And I said,

"No problem! Consider it done." I'm not even going to speculate why talk about his women was off limits. That's what Suge wanted, that's what I did.

It wasn't out of fear, it was out of respect. That was his only request: Granted. He was truthful about everything else and willing to talk about anything else. So I respected his one wish.

Suge commands that kind of respect. He carries himself in such a way that you get the feeling that he fears nothing and no one.

My husband and I were in Miami riding down the street in a convertible. We were on Collins Avenue just chilling. We get to a light and look over and on a motorcycle next to our car is Suge Knight. He has a woman on the back of his bike and he's just chilling—no helmet, no protection.

I tell this story because it highlights for me who Suge Knight is—a man who seems to love danger, seems to not shy away from anything, riding around on a motorcycle without a helmet. It also underscores how comfortable and free he is. In an industry where bodyguards and entourages are part of the tools of the trade, here was Suge Knight in the middle of Miami, just him and his chick on a bike. He had been out of jail maybe a couple of months, but he didn't seem to have a care in the world.

Our chance meeting on the streets of Miami turned into us exchanging information and staying in touch with one another.

Suge Knight is a very touchy subject for me. I am proud of the interviews that I have done with him, both for the *Experience* and for VH1. I am flattered that he considers my gangsta like his—but on a different level. And I appreciate that he respects what I do. The feeling is mutual.

But Suge Knight is not to be messed with. I am happy I am on his good side. At the end of the day, you're damn right I don't want to be on his bad side. Not that I did a lot to get on his good side. But when you're on his bad side . . .

SK: *I can get along with anybody, and I can sit down and take it to the next level. Except for a snitch and a rat. Snoop [Doggy Dogg] is a snitch. [Dr.] Dre is a rat.*

WW: *If you saw Snoop in the club, would you splash champagne on him? Would you sic him, would you—*

SK: *I wouldn't splash champagne on nobody. But, I'mma tell you like this. Even if I wanted to, I don't think the champagne would go that far, fast as he can run.* (Laughs.)

WW: *Are you still pounding Negroes? Is that still part of your MO? Because you know the legendary stories with, who was the white rapper, the man that you were alleged to have hung [out of a window] by his feet? Vanilla Ice?*

SK: *Unh-huh.*

WW: *And all like that. The Andre Harrell story at Uptown Records. You trapped the little man in the bathroom and made him squeal. I mean, is that still a part of your gangster—*

SK: *I look at it like this: I'm not gonna sit up here and do no lying. I'm not gonna sit up here and be like trying to say what I did and what I didn't do.*

WW: *Okay.*

SK: *Certain things I wouldn't talk about what I did; it's just not smart talking about it.*

WW: *Right.*

SK: *One of the things that I always believed in, I believed in taking care of my people. It's like right now I meet you and I like your style and you walked outside and somebody brought harm to you—*

WW: *Mmm-hmm.*

SK: *—I would defend you.*

WW: *Okay.*

SK: *By all means necessary.*

WW: *Okay.*

SK: *I would definitely go hard.*

WW: *Go hard. Hmmm.*

SK: *So, if that makes me a bad person, that makes me a bad person. I'm not the type of guy to prey on the weak, though.*

WW: *I got you.*

SK: *I have never been a type of guy that was a bully who picked on the little kids after school. I always picked on the big kids.*

WW: *Okay.*

SK: *So, you know, [there's] a difference.*

WW: *Yeah, there is.*

SK: *It's a big difference. And all the people who [are] telling on you supposed to be so-called, wannabe thugs, but they street punks. If you really look at it, in your music, in your interviews, you speak of yourself one way, but when it's dealing with me you [are] totally opposite because you [are] telling the police on me.*

WW: *Right.*

SK: *You're putting statements against me.*

WW: *Right, right. Okay.*

SK: *You acting like hos.*

WW: *Okay, okay.*

SK: *I don't understand that part.*

WW: *Okay.*

SK: *You know, that's the part that's really, I wouldn't say*

bothering me, it's just a big disappointment. You know, if
we gonna do it, let's do it. If you come swing on me, I'm
definitely gonna swing on you.
WW: *Okay.*
SK: *And we gonna deal with it like that. But after I put my*
foot in your ass, don't turn around and then wanna
sue me.

The dark side of Suge Knight is not just hearsay or braggado-
cio on his part. His dark side is well chronicled.

In 1994, Suge was convicted of beating two musicians with a
telephone at his Death Row studios. The next year trouble followed him to a party that he attended, where a man was beaten
to death. No one was arrested. That same year at a Christmas
party in Beverly Hills, Suge was accused of forcing a noted label
executive—alleged to have been Andre Harrell—to drink urine
from a champagne glass after Harrell allegedly refused to give up
the address of Janice Combs, the mother of Puffy Combs. Suge
says this didn't happen, and no one was arrested.

In September of 1996, Suge was driving a car near the Las Vegas strip. In the passenger seat was Suge's number-one artist,
Tupac Shakur. There was a drive-by shooting. Tupac was mur-
dered. His killer and the circumstances surrounding his death
are still a mystery. Suge went to jail that year for violating parole
stemming from his 1994 assault conviction. He was caught on
tape along with Tupac, hours before the fatal drive-by shooting,
participating in a beat-down of a member of the Crips gang in a
Vegas casino. He was sentenced to nine years in prison.

While Suge was in jail, Christopher "The Notorious B.I.G.,"
aka "Biggie" Wallace, was gunned down in Los Angeles. Suge was

investigated for this murder. A car that was linked to the murder was found at Suge's house. The investigation was dropped due to lack of evidence.

WW: *Okay. So how do you feel about people still looking at you as the cause of Biggie's death? Tupac's death? You know?*

SK: *I look at it like real simple. For somebody to say I had anything to do with both of those deaths is absolutely crazy. We got to weed out a lot of jealousy, though. Because, I'm my own man. I do my own thing. I don't bother nobody, but I don't run from no shit.*

WW: *Right.*

SK: *And the thing is, as far as Pac, everybody knew how I felt about Pac. Everybody knew how Pac felt about me.*

WW: *Mmm-hmm.*

SK: *And the thing is that in the Pac situation, I actually pulled him down.*

WW: *Mmm-hmm.*

SK: *And got, I got hit in the head.*

WW: *Where were you hit in the head?*

SK: *Uhhh?*

WW: *Like do you still have a scar or anything like that?*

SK: *You can feel it. A big lump. That's the injury to my skull.*

WW: *Yeah.*

SK: *And one of the things about it: When they found it . . . first I was supposed to been in a bad situation. When they found out it was me they tried to say it like it was a fragment or graze or whatever.*

WW: *Ohh.*

SK: *Because, you know, one thing about black people, if you're in power they wanna destroy you, slander your name, or*

46

say a whole bunch of stuff. So, anybody, ANYBODY, anybody with any sense, anybody that really knew Pac, knew I cared about Pac more than anybody—even his own people.

WW: *How is your relationship with Afeni Shakur, and then we'll talk about Voletta Wallace.*

SK: *Right. My relationship with Afeni is, I look at it like she's a mother. I know I heard a lot of things when I was in prison. We had a conversation, and the deal that Pac had with Interscope was a deal where he would never in life make money.*

WW: *Yeah.*

SK: *The deal he did with me was an incredible, incredible, incredible deal. So therefore, even when I was in prison and I heard they were trying to say, well he had [a] bad deal with Death Row, he had this great deal with Interscope. I said okay, well, if that was the case let's chuck the Death Row contract and go with the Interscope contract.*

WW: *Okay.*

SK: *'Cause on the Interscope contract he was getting like, I don't know point for point, but maybe after it's all said and done, three points, seven points, like that.*

WW: *Okay.*

SK: *Death Row, he was getting up to twenty points. Big difference.*

WW: *So you're saying that your relationship then with Afeni Shakur is respectable and—*

SK: *Right, right. And then Interscope was charging them a hundred percent on videos. If he spent a million dollars on a video, he'll pay a million dollars. With me, if he spent a million dollars, I pay half, he pay half.*

WW: *Okay, okay.*

SK: *So, I gave him an incredible superstar deal.*

WW: *Right.*

SK: *But as usual, people gonna look at me because I'm from the ghetto—*

WW: *Mmm-hmm.*

SK: *—that I'm doing a bad deal with him.*

WW: *Yeah.*

SK: *And since these other guys is not from the ghetto, they're doing—*

WW: *The white people.*

SK: *Yeah. It's a difference. Plain as day. You know, majority of slave mentalities think that white people's ice is colder than black people's ice—*

WW: *Right.*

In 2000, while still serving time for probation violation, according to a published report, he donated twenty-one thousand dollars to rebuild a Sacramento, California, playground for children from low-income families. Suge helped replace a jungle gym with carousels, swings, and monkey bars that had been destroyed by vandals who set it on fire.

He was quoted as saying: "I saw a report about it on local TV. A playground is the only safe place for kids to play, and then somebody comes along and destroys it. A senseless crime that hurts little kids. I called Death Row Records in Los Angeles, told them to find out the cost to rebuild the playground, and cut a check to cover it."

Such is the dichotomy that is Suge Knight. He is a man with an enormous capacity to do good things. He is also a man with a very dark side as well.

In a published report following the acquittal of Puffy of those gun and bribery charges stemming from the shooting at Club New York in 1999, Suge is quoted as saying: "They don't send a nigga who's wearing shiny suits and hanging out with Martha Stewart to jail. Who is he a threat to? He's just acting a fool. I'm the nigga people are afraid of."

And he ain't lied yet.

And Suge doesn't bite his tongue in regards to Puffy. He made no bones about his disdain for the way Puffy let Shyne take the full rap for that Club New York shooting:

WW: *So, the rumor has it that you're in New York because you're trying to get Shyne the way you got Tupac. Is there any truth to that? Which, by the way, would be a brilliant plan. I mean, it would free the man from jail light years before he would actually get out.*

SK: *Actually, I would bail the guy out. I would do what I can to get that guy out. He don't necessarily have to be an artist on Tha Row, but I would do it because I think that was like one of the worst things that could happen to anybody. That's when I had a little, little, little, little respect, very little respect for Puffy. The little respect was 'cause he's black. After what he did to Shyne—*

WW: *He snitched. Right?*

SK: *He's a rat. I do not like rats. I do not like snitches. I think a rat is the lowest that you can get.*

WW: *Yeah.*

SK: *I think any snitches or rats are in the way. I think they should either be the ones not living and let somebody else live who wanna make a difference, or they should be the ones locked up and let the ones who try to do something outta prison. The thing about it is that what Puffy did was very, very wrong. That broke all rules. But, more importantly, if that was my artist—*

WW: *Mmm-hmm.*

SK: *—and they was gonna give him ten years, knowing that the judge, they really want me, and he had this old Hollywood-ass lawyer, he had Johnnie Cochran—*

WW: *Yeah, yeah, yeah.*

SK: *I'da went to Johnnie and said, "Look, they trying to give him ten years, they really want me, tell 'em we'll do a deal. I'll do a year, Shyne do a year, and we'll walk."*

WW: *Okay.*

SK: *And I think they woulda went for it. They woulda went for it.*

WW: *You know, Suge, not for nothing, that is a pretty damn good plan right there.*

SK: *They woulda went for it. And I woulda did a year for my artist. I woulda did two years or even three, but he coulda got away with doing a year. They coulda did a year apiece.*

WW: *So have you put any money in Shyne's commissary and have you been to visit him?*

SK: *I haven't been to visit him. I mean, they ain't gonna let me go visit him. I am on parole. . . .*

WW: *Oh, that's right.* (Laughs.)

SK: (Chuckles.) *You know? But I sent the word out there and you know, if he wanna holla, he'll holla at me and I'll holla back. You know? And as far as putting money on his books, that's nothing. I'm trying to get the boy a lawyer to get him up outta there for he can have a career.*

WW: *Wow.*

Suge is back in jail for violating probation stemming from the beating of a parking lot attendant. He's away now, but he will be back. Dudes like Suge don't just go away . . . silently. He'll be back. Whether he will be putting out good music or terrorizing the game when he's out is the question. But he will be back.

I look forward to Suge coming back. Hip-hop needs Suge because in hip-hop you almost have to take it—take whatever it is that you want—or you're not going to get it. And there are so many snakes in the game that the game needs someone whose foot is big enough to stomp on the heads of the snakes, or least let the snakes know that the foot is out there. He balances the game.

In an industry full of devils, you need to have one devil that even the other devils fear. You need one person whom people can turn to. That people are scared of Suge—and make no mistake, even the biggest names and the so-called baddest people in hip-hop are afraid of Suge—is a good thing.

But with that fear comes responsibility.

CHAPTER

3

What Happened to Hip-Hop?

I remember when hip-hop traded in its African medallions and gold chains for Glocks and a gangsta mentality. It was in the early 1990s, and I didn't like it at all. I went from going to appearances at clubs where everyone was raising their glasses in glee as they sang along with Naughty by Nature's "Hip Hop Hooray" to making sure I had security at all times and constantly watching the exit doors to be certain that I could get out in a hurry just in case. I would even see that if we parked in a lot, it would not be the one closest to the venue, because in a fast getaway I didn't want to be where the crowd was. Hip-hop turned dangerous in the mid 1990s for no particular reason.

In many ways, I guess, hip-hop was mirroring society at the time. People were getting shot and stabbed for simply stepping on someone's new sneakers by accident. Crack and drug dealing in neighborhoods made drive-bys and other violence one more thing to worry about. But I expected more out of hip-hop. It not only was the voice for what was happening, but the hip-hop that I grew up with, in many ways, *shaped* what would happen. It was the Pied Piper for social change.

But gangsta rap, which took the place of the consciousness of acts like Public Enemy, A Tribe Called Quest, KRS-One, and the fun of De La Soul, Heavy D & the Boyz, and Digital Underground, and the sassiness of Salt-N-Pepa, seemed to become the dominant voice—or at least the voice that the record labels were putting out the money for.

There was more rapping about guns and drugs and less rapping about things that would make you think.

It was funny to watch Tupac Shakur, who many people forget was down with that Humpty dude with the big nose and all of the Digital Underground shenanigans, go from a fun-loving little guy from New York to this West Coast gangsta rapper. When did all of that happen? Didn't he start off rapping about how he got around?

I remember when the only battles in rap took place on the airwaves and on records. I actually remember getting all caught up in the Roxanne Shante-versus-the-world drama in the late 1980s and early 1990s. Remember Roxanne Shante and all of those battles with everyone from UTFO to JJ Fad to the Real Roxanne to Sparky Dee? Those battles were silly and fun. No one got hurt—except for a few feelings—and it energized rap in a way where people paid attention.

Even serious rappers like LL Cool J were known to get into a few scuffles. He had it out with Kool Moe Dee (whatever happened to him?), Ice-T (whose rap career fell off so much that he had to focus his energies on acting), and Canibus (who has seemingly fallen completely off the face of the earth and must be in a witness protection program somewhere).

And after nearly twenty years in the game, LL Cool J is still standing. And I dare someone to come after him and try to verbally battle him even today. He has vanquished all in his path and he did it on his records—not in the streets, not with violence. He kept the beefing where it belonged—on the songs. And LL's battles are among the most memorable. Note to young rappers looking to make a name for themselves by going after vets: Make sure the vet doesn't have real lyrical skills. That's why, in my opinion, LL is the GOAT.

But somewhere in hip-hop, beefs became real and guns and the threat of violence became real. And I'm not quite sure when it turned or how. I don't believe there was an East Coast versus West Coast thing that led to it. I think it was more personal than that. And I do believe that Suge and Puffy and the nastiness between the two were at the crux of the mess that developed.

Even the names of record labels began to tell the tale. We went from Def Jam and Rhino Records and Uptown and Tommy Boy to Bad Boy, Death Row, and later Murder Inc. The record label heads, who were once these white men from corporate America, became thugs from the street. They brought their street mentality and their street rules to the game and changed it—for the worst.

Tupac versus Biggie. I don't even understand this beef. I don't think these men, if left on their own and not sucked into someone else's nastiness, would have even had a problem with each other. They were friends. But a lot of "he said, he said" and lies and innuendoes eventually led to the murder of them both. How sad.

I got a telephone call from Los Angeles in the middle of the night. The caller said Biggie had just been shot outside of a club. He was in L.A. for the Soul Train Music Awards. This was before it hit the news outlets. I had been invited to the awards show, as I am every year, but I didn't go that year.

The death of Biggie affected me because it was very close.

Biggie was New York. And Biggie didn't seem to be really a part of that whole gangsta movement, but somehow he was caught up in the game and he lost his life. He wasn't like Tupac, who seemed to be almost looking for trouble and who had been in fights and been shot before.

Somehow Biggie ended up dead, and I can't really explain why. And it had an impact on me—professionally and personally. That was a light-bulb moment for me.

It let me know that the danger in the game was real. No longer could I simply go to these events, go to the after-parties, and not give a second thought to my safety. In fact, it changed a lot of what I do. While invited to major events in hip-hop, I rarely attend. And if I do attend a Soul Train Award or Lady of Soul or Source Award show, I don't go in. I do the red carpet and I'm out—no after-parties, no hanging out, nothing. I won't even stay in the same hotel or even in the same part of town as the event planners and the eventgoers.

Mostly, I stay in New York and receive feeds from others. I tell my moles, "You go and call me and let me know what you see." Between that and listeners who frequent these events, I get my information just fine. I don't have to be in the piece to be in the know. I get reports from all different perspectives.

I even have hotel workers who are informants to things going down. By the way, some hotel and airport workers have opened my eyes to a whole new hustle in the hip-hop game. You have read about how rappers like Ludacris and Lil' Kim have been ripped off big time when traveling. Well, there is a whole game out there to rip off rappers, and it has become too easy. People who work in these industries know when an event is popping off. They know who all is going to be there too. If they work inside of the hotel, they know the room and they have the key and they know these stars travel heavy—with all of their cash and jewels and expensive gear. They know they will find the best Versace, the Cartier bracelets, the alligator shoes, the Gucci, the Louis, the ice, and the platinum. Because if you're a star in hip-hop, you cannot afford to be seen without your finest shit (unless you're a dirty backpacker and don't care about material things).

So people at the airports know these stars are traveling and they know they can't carry on everything. So luggage is mysteriously missing along with its contents. In the hotels, they also know because many of these stars don't keep their things in the hotel safe. And many are plotted on and set up for weeks in advance. I'm getting my information straight from people who work in the hotels. There are maids and other hotel workers who look forward to these awards shows and Hollywood premieres—it's like a second job for them. And the payoff can be big.

And traveling from one coast to another is also the best time to get got physically. People know, if you're coming from the East Coast to an award show in Los Angeles, that you aren't traveling with a gun—unless you have people in Los Angeles looking out. For the most part, if you have some beef with someone, going to an award show makes you somewhat of a sitting duck. Security didn't save Biggie.

Word has it that everybody is vulnerable these days. This has less to do with hip-hop and more to do with the state of where we are as a country right now. The state of thirst. Everybody wants to live the life. They see Queen Latifah giving her business partner a four-hundred-thousand-dollar Rolls-Royce Phantom for his birthday and Oprah giving one to Stevie Wonder just for performing at her fiftieth birthday party (of course, he'll need a driver), and people want one too. They see this and they'll do anything for it.

They see on TV all of the reality shows and the *MTV Cribs*es and the *How I'm Livings* on BET. Hell, even *The Real World* presents the life with those big-ass decked-out luxury houses that those kids stay in. That life is right there for people to grab, or so it seems. It's out of reach for most. But they still thirst for it and are willing to do whatever they can to get it.

I have mixed feelings about the messages shows like *Cribs* and BET's *How I'm Living* send. On one hand, I am pleased when I watch how some people are using their money today. *Cribs* is a wonderful introduction into our culture, because it is making our artists spend their money on the American dream—which is home ownership.

There was a time when we did not know how artists lived. So they could still live in the projects and have three Benzes and all the jewelry and a big knot of money in their pocket and own nothing—still renting.

With the invention of *Cribs,* home ownership and all of the accoutrements attached to a house are things everyone wants. It's competition now with the artists. And I believe it helps young people in general aspire to something higher than just having the "iced-out" chains and the cars they see in videos. Now young people want home ownership too. They just have to figure out how to do it.

What *Cribs* doesn't explain is the process of owning a home. It doesn't take you through the mortgage process or having credit. They don't tell you that if you purchase a home with cash, you have to pay the taxes *every* year—even the years you aren't making money. It doesn't explain that some of these homes are actually rented or owned by the record label—not the artist. A lot of these artists who seem to own a house don't technically own a house. Suge Knight has been known to purchase houses in

Death Row's name for his artists. I was talking to Snoop Doggy Dogg and he told me that's how it went down when he was on the label. All along you think you own something and you don't own anything at all. When the recording career is over, they could walk away with absolutely nothing. It's a shame that some of these artists are too stupid to question things like "Why am I not signing anything? Why haven't I gone to a closing?"

Cribs would be doing these people a real service if it would devote a show to the process of obtaining some of these homes and boats and cars, etc. But they don't. They just show all of the fabulousness of how people are living and they leave those who aren't living that way wanting it. Wanting it all.

And this feeling goes beyond hip-hop and celebrity. This is about people in general. People want what they see other people have. But in hip-hop, there seems to be a deeper hunger, a deeper thirst. Perhaps it is because many view the stars of the game as being no better than they are. These are regular people who got a break somehow. They come out of the same projects or from the same neighborhoods as many in the streets, and folks look at them and say, "Why them?" or "They are nothing special!" It's that attitude, and the jealousy that accompanies it, that are extremely dangerous. And as a result, many in the game cannot travel back to their old neighborhood without the fear of being robbed or followed or worse.

Summer is probably one of the most dangerous times of year in the urban community, because that is when people are out and things are in your face—the drop-tops are visible, the cars are shining, the jewels are blinging. And people, who are just not even thinking about the dangers with their tops down, windows down, and rims spinning, are vulnerable. Folks see the nice cars, they see chrome spinning on rims, and they want to know how they can get it. And the easiest way is to simply take it. It makes the block very savage. People are very, very thirsty.

And what's worse is to have a taste of that life and lose it. That thirst is even greater. After the Lost Boyz broke up and Mr. Cheeks went on to find solo success, the rest of the group was left out in the cold. But they had grown accustomed to a certain lifestyle that was no longer there.

Ronald Blackwell, aka Spigg Nice, of the Lost Boyz, resorted to bank robbing. He did more than a dozen bank robberies all over New Jersey. He was finally caught, and in January of 2004 Spigg Nice was sentenced to thirty-seven years in a federal prison and was ordered to pay $994,478 in joint restitution. Damn, was it worth it? And in federal prison there is no parole, no time off for good behavior. He will be serving thirty-seven years.

The last time I saw Spigg Nice was at a party in 2002 in New York City. It was in the middle of winter. I remember him because he looked so fabulous. I knew he wasn't making that Lost Boyz money, but he was sporting a full-length white mink coat, and had all the ice and platinum trimmings to go along with the mink. He looked like he was doing the damn thing. And I was wondering how he was keeping up. He had the diamonds, the haircut, the look.

It's competitive out there. And people do some crazy things— like bank robbing and even carjacking—to stay in the game.

John Forte, of the Fugees, seemingly had it all. And somehow that still wasn't enough. Here was a guy from Brownsville, Brooklyn, who got a full scholarship to attend upscale, lily-white Phillips Exeter Academy in New Hampshire. He went to New York University, where he studied music, before leaving for the music business. He hooked up with the Fugees and was nominated for a Grammy. He had even dropped a solo album.

But in the winter of 2002, John Forte was caught with thirty-one pounds of cocaine worth one and a half million dollars. And today is serving fourteen years for possession with intent to distribute. John Forte, aka inmate No. 88840-079, is yet another victim of the trappings of this game. The thirst seems unquenchable to many. And it's so sad.

In 2004, star football player Jamal Lewis, of the Baltimore Ravens, was indicted and charged with conspiring to possess with the intent to distribute five kilograms of cocaine. And not only are rappers and athletes getting into the drug game to stay ahead, but the drug game has totally commandeered much of rap. How many rappers, from Jay-Z to 50 Cent, have admitted to coming from the drug game? And there are many unnamed, behind-the-scenes executives who have made quite an easy transition from the streets who are now heading up rap labels. It's getting scary.

The problem in hip-hop is that even within the game there are the haves and the have-nots. There are really only a handful of artists who are actually making the real money. Now, don't get me wrong, there are a lot more millionaires in the game today than there were fifteen, twenty years ago when hip-hop was just starting. Today you might find those in hip-hop out at the Hamptons partying with Robert De Niro. Hip-hop wasn't doing that fifteen years ago. How fabulous is that? If you have the right money, you're now living next door to Robert De Niro in the Hamptons and that is one of your many homes. That's fabulous too. There are more moguls and more moguls doing the right things with their money today in hip-hop than ever before. These moguls—like Russell Simmons, Puffy, Damon Dash—are sending their kids to these thirty-five-thousand-dollar-a-year private schools in Manhattan. And I think it's great. I think it's great that the moguls are buying coveted New York City property and we see it on *MTV Cribs*. They even have trust funds for their kids. There is a generation now who will be actually leaving something for the next generation.

I've also noticed there are still just as many men being sloppy with the penis, which has led to the downfall of some of these moguls. Having babies with different women and being sloppy with the unprotected sex can be very costly.

There are a lot of sad stories that we don't find out about until so much later. I was really shocked when TLC talked about being broke after having had so much success. They are the consummate example of a very successful group—they sold millions upon millions of records and seemed to be living the high life—who really had nothing. Their story underscores the nastiness and some of the realities of this business.

I remember them on VH1 and the late Lisa "Left Eye" Lopez, telling all about how they were broke—selling ten million records and being broke. She talked about how they only got something like fifty thousand dollars apiece after *Ooh ... on the TLC Tip* went multiplatinum. And that money included all of the touring they did that year. And Chili and T-Boz were sitting there cosigning everything Left Eye was saying. It was so sad to hear. And even sadder that their manager, Pebbles, was behind it all. Shut up! That rings in my head so loud, and those girls were so busy having fun and so busy trusting Pebbles that they weren't watching their bottom line.

Sometimes we feel as though we're protected when we're watched over by a big sister or a mother figure or someone with the same skin tone, if you know what I mean.

You'd be surprised at how many people are out here giving

you the illusion of the life who really don't have it at all. And you'd be surprised at the number of people who have all of the cars and all of the things but don't even have life insurance—the basic things. You're supposed to have life insurance or money set aside for your kids that you cannot touch even if the bottom were to drop out.

It's very important. Even in my career, I feel that this can be over any day. In entertainment, whether you're on the radio or a platinum-selling artist, you can make—and not everyone does—a lot of money fast. And the most important thing about making fast money is acknowledging that it can be over tomorrow, just as fast. You must always have in the back of your mind a Plan B. It is very Negroidian not to have a backup plan and to only live for today.

You need a plan for either how you're going to maintain your lavish lifestyle or how you will adjust emotionally to scaling back. It could be quite tragic for people to be living in a big house one day and then having to get a little condo, or renting a little apartment, tomorrow.

Everybody has Gucci dreams, but you have to have everything very well thought out. And it goes beyond getting a business manager—somebody telling you what to do with your money and your time and your future. When in actuality *you* should have a plan of your own.

I learned through trial and error how to make do with the money I've been making. I never had a bunch of money to blow. Even during the time I was caught up in my cocaine addiction, I didn't have all this money I was blowing. And cocaine was so cheap that it wasn't making me broke. Where did I learn this? Being paranoid and cheap.

Having a baby really put things in perspective. I didn't have life insurance before I had little Kevin, because it was just me and my husband. And I believe a grown man should continue to work if, God forbid, something happened to me. I had life insurance through my job. I didn't get the big policy where they come to your house and take blood and weigh you and all of that, I didn't have that until I had my child. I didn't need that before. You're not going to kill me for the life insurance money.

Life insurance is particularly important in terms of making sure that your children are okay. That was a conscious effort for me. Now that we have little Kevin, we have life insurance, a college fund. And I even have a fuck-you fund for me. This is separate from my son's money. I promised myself that we would never go into his college fund for anything. If things got tough and we couldn't pay the mortgage, that's our fault. I would never jeopardize our son's future. I don't want to ruin it for him. He didn't ask to be born to these two idiot parents who tricked up all of the money.

I wish more people would take care of their money and take care of their future. Just as easy as it came, it can go. If you're riding high today, you can be rock bottom tomorrow. So prepare, prepare, prepare, for the worst. And stop chasing after things that really are not important in the long run.

I wonder how far things are going to go in hip-hop. There is a movement afoot to bring it back to the original flavor. There are some new artists who seem to want to bring the fun back. With the emergence of groups like OutKast, who are moving hip-hop into a whole other realm, there is hope. I pump my fists for Out-Kast. And Missy Elliott is always coming with something original and fun. And there is Kanye West as well. But the industry seems to reward those with gangsta. Artists like 50 Cent and his bulletproof vests seem to get the attention of the labels. Hopefully this will change.

Ultimately, it is up to the people to change by sending a message with their purchasing habits. The people will have the last word on where hip-hop ends up.

CHAPTER
4
The Elvis Factor

The first multiplatinum rap album? The Beastie Boys' *License to Ill*. It was the top-selling rap album of the 1980s. Vanilla Ice debuted his album *To the Extreme* in 1991, and it became the top-selling album of all time. It sold seven million copies in its first year in the United States alone. And it held the title of top-selling rap album until Eminem knocked it out of the box a decade later.

Eminem is now the top rapper in the game, with Grammys, movies, and even an Academy Award for best song.

What's wrong with this picture?

Well, if you are a rapper in the game who has been struggling to just get your songs heard, a lot is wrong. If you are a pioneer who helped shape and mold what rap and hip-hop are today, there is plenty wrong with this picture. If you are a young person growing up in an urban neighborhood for which rap and hip-hop are the means through which your voice is heard, this picture is completely wrong.

Seeing the emergence of white rappers is bittersweet. The success of the Beastie Boys, Vanilla Ice—whose *To the Extreme* was the first rap album to sell more than seven million copies—and now Eminem has brought a level of legitimacy to rap and hip-hop. It has brought financial success and has broadened the appeal and the marketplace for many rappers. It has made rap and hip-hop cross over in a way that could be very positive for this country. It is a rallying point for many of the young and bridges many social, racial, and economic gaps. That's all good.

But at the same time, all of this progress has happened at the expense of the very people who created the music in the first place.

Eminem is in the *Guinness Book of World Records* for being the fastest-selling rap artist in history, for his *Marshall Mathers LP*. That the names of these people can be in record books and that they can go down in history as being the most successful rappers of all time can possibly undermine all of the work that was done by the true pioneers. Years from now, when all of us are gone and all that is left are record books, future generations may actually believe that the Beastie Boys and Eminem propelled rap and hip-hop to another height. They could be viewed as the pioneers of the game.

The truth is that in this game, white sells. We saw it with Elvis back in the day and we see it with Eminem today. If a white person can emulate a black person and white people get to enjoy the music without looking at the black face associated with it, then they can be a huge success—even more successful than the blacks they emulate. The Beatles—biggest group of the millennium—admittedly borrowed from the sounds of people like Little Richard. Most of Elvis's hits were written by black men, and his sound was definitely "soulful."

In music today you have Justin Timberlake, who is the most soulful white boy alive. They even had him hosting the 45th Anniversary of Motown.

This makes many people furious. Few rappers, for fear of industry backlash, will talk about this openly or loudly. Ray Benzino, a rapper and co-owner of the *Source* magazine, has been on a crusade. He has been accused of hating and he is hating—hating how the game is going. He and Eminem had a well-documented battle in 2003. Benzino's *Source* magazine exposed some racist lyrics Eminem spit on a song before he blew up about a black girl he used to date. And the two men exchanged harsh lyrics in songs.

Benzino, in my opinion, really cares about the state and future of hip-hop. He is someone who has taken it upon himself to speak out about things no one else seems willing or able to speak out about. He has put a bull's-eye around Eminem as the poster boy for what ails hip-hop. And whether he is right or not, his discussion is at least something hip-hop needs to hear. He's not talking about taking out Glocks and blowing people away, he's talking about taking back hip-hop and not selling out to the "machine."

Ray Benzino (RB): I got nothing against white rappers. Anybody should be able to rap. Black, white, purple, blue. You just gotta be true to yourself and recognize the hood and you a'ight with me.

Wendy Williams (WW): Okay.

RB: You know again, it really isn't ... Eminem just brings it out more, I think.

WW: Right.

RB: I think this is an issue that is bigger than Eminem. You know, my whole situation with Eminem was really brought up just to bring light that the hood ain't selling units no more and that there's a problem with big corporations and

*the other culture trying to take our culture and just run
with it, man, and just, you know, today it seems like I'm
the only one who's spoke up for that. As far as, you know,
artists are concerned. But you can best believe all the
artists are gonna reap, you know what I'm saying?*

WW: *Do you find that behind closed doors many artists agree
with what you're saying? It's just that they may not have
the backbone to come out and speak about it?*

RB: *That's crazy to me. Because if you can find time to beef
with each other, you definitely should find time to talk
about a situation that's really bad for the whole culture.
And a lot of times, you know, like we're blinded. It's that
whole divide-and-conquer theory, you know what I'm saying? As long as we're going at each other, then you really
don't focus on the real problem. But you know, I've seen it
coming.*

WW: *Right.*

RB: *I had the blessings basically to see hip-hop from the inside
and outside.*

WW: *Uh-huh.*

RB: *And, you know, I've basically come from the streets of Rox-
bury, Dorchester, Massachusetts. I came up in a time, very
violent time—gang, drugs, guns—and, you know, survived
that. Very proud that I survived that. And helped a lot of
my guys survive it and, you know, I just, it's just . . . you
know, I go all across the country and I'm in the neighborhoods and it's just sad to see a lot of these kids, basically,
really putting they everything into this rhyming and it's
just like they're not getting a chance to be heard or, you
know what I'm saying, it's just not right. Right now, the
game's nasty.*

WW: *But you know a lot of people, um, Benzino, are saying that the reason you're upset is because you're not selling—*

RB: *Uh-huh.*

WW: *—the same units as an Eminem or somebody of that nature.*

RB: *There's no way that anybody is gonna be able to sell the units that Eminem [sells]. . . . I've accepted that.*

WW: *Right.*

RB: *I've been into this game for the love. "Rock the Party" is the biggest song of my career and, you know, it was a situation I was in Miami then the 8 Mile [Eminem] thing came out. It just was just too much for me to take. And I felt like hip-hop is, you should be able to use it as a tool to bring social consciousness, and I felt that this was a topic that created social consciousness. You know, I didn't get into it to wage any type of war, you know, a race war, because it's not racial. One thing about hip-hop is that it's bridged those racial gaps, man, you know what I'm saying? Hip-hop is a great thing. I think the people that was against hip-hop from the start didn't like the way it bridged the racial gaps—*

WW: *Right.*

RB: *—and I think this is the way that they can basically push the streets and separate hip-hop. You know, I been doing interviews and, man, you have white radio personalities all across the country who do morning shows who just started playing hip-hop and getting into hip-hop.*

WW: *Right.*

RB: *These are the same people who never wanted to be involved with hip-hop.*

WW: *Right.*

71

RB: *But now just because Eminem is, you know, perceived to be number one . . .*

WW: *Right.*

RB: *They're embracing him and it's like they're going against me just because.*

WW: *Right.*

RB: *It hasn't, like, they had no real point.*

WW: *Right.*

RB: *You understand what I'm saying? They don't see what's going on and they really don't care. And I be getting a lot of that till, really, you know, you, a lot of people are being exposed as far as, if their, to me their true colors show when they start talking about hip-hop and, you know, and how Eminem is the king of hip-hop and, you know, basically I can be the whipping boy. It's no problem. I'm built for this, Wendy. You know what I'm saying?*

I do. When Benzino compares Eminem to what is going on today, a lot of people look at him as raging and bitter because he doesn't have his own platinum line on his walls and Eminem does. But I understand where he is coming from. Rock and roll was started by blacks. But when you look at rock and roll today, it is a white thing and it appears to have always been a white thing.

The most successful hip-hop radio stations in the country are owned by whites. My station, WBLS—one of the last of a dying breed of black-owned radio stations—isn't exactly ringing the loudest bells (outside of the *Experience,* of course). We are the station at the end of the dial, the little station that could. And I am proud to say that I am working for a black-owned radio station. It is the second time in my career that I am getting my money from a black situation, and I've never had any checks bounce. Kathy Hughes's Radio One was the other black-owned entity that I worked for. And Radio One, the largest black-owned radio conglomerate in the country, doesn't even own the most urban stations in this country—white-run Clear Channel does.

I see that if things continue where there was one white rapper after the other, rap music and its artists would evolve into something that would have white rappers as the greatest rappers of all times. And they would all follow in the steps of Eminem with platinum hits, crossover success, great endorsement deals, movies, etc.

Of course, the black rappers want all of these things too. They all want a successful television sitcom, an Oscar nomination, Grammys lined up.

I know where Benzino is coming from. And when we talked in 2003 he said nothing that surprised me. He's down with hip-hop. He feels it's empty, it's void. But that happens when things go corporate and that happens when things have to be managed.

WW: *Do you think that Eminem is a culture stealer?*

RB: *I believe the people . . . I think he's the puppet. For sure. I believe that he might've started into this just, you know, like everybody else. He loves hip-hop, wants to be involved with it, but then once the puppet masters start pulling the strings—*

WW: *Right.*

RB: *—I think that he just started going along with it. You know, every article he's frowning . . . he has a doo-rag on.*

WW: *Yeah. Right.*

RB: *He has a skully on. Like, come on. Like, you know what I mean? Since when? You came into this game as Slim Shady, you know, cross-dressing and—*

WW: *Right.*

RB: *—being the funny guy.*

WW: *Right, right.*

RB: *Now all of a sudden he's gangsta.*

WW: *Yeah. He's got a clothing line coming out too. Slim Shady Wear.*

RB: *Slim Shady Wear?*

WW: *Yeah.*

RB: *I mean, you know what? That's a smart business move, because as big as his brand is, of course he's gonna want to expand it. So, I can't be mad at that. It's just that, is it good for our culture?*

What we do know is that corporate America and Madison Avenue are heavily influenced by hip-hop—just turn on your television and check for the commercials.

Now you have pundits and talk show hosts like Bill O'Reilly talking about it and coming down on corporations who support certain rappers. In 2002, Bill O'Reilly, on his *O'Reilly Factor,* began a campaign targeting Ludacris and his endorsement of products like Pepsi. He called for a boycott of Pepsi for being "immoral" for allowing a "gangsta rapper" like Ludacris, whose lyrics are damaging to society, to endorse its product. After that, Pepsi fired Ludacris as a spokesperson. That's powerful.

And as long as corporate America can turn from Ludacris to Justin Timberlake and affect the same people, then it will. And if rappers want to satisfy corporate America, then they have to water down what they put out. You're damned if you do, damned if you don't. If you keep it too real, then you have to answer to corporate America because it's frightening to the masses.

Rapping about a Maybach Benz is keeping it real for the 50 Cents, the Jay-Zs, and the Ja Rules. For others, rapping about murder, murder, kill, kill, may be keeping it real too. But if you're rhyming about Glocks and killing, don't expect to be the new face of Tommy. That's real too. While keeping it real sells, it's a lot easier to sell it when the face of the salesman is less threatening.

WW: *I don't see where the hood is really buying Eminem music. I think that is the rest of America that is buying Eminem music.*

RB: *But once we stamp him, that's when it's okay for, you know, the rest. . . . See, 'cause everybody watches what we do.*

WW: *Right.*

RB: *Make no mistake. The way we dress, what we drive, how we talk.*

WW: *Yes.*

RB: *They watch what we do because it's in our culture, our blood, to bring this, you know what I'm saying?*

WW: *Yes, yes.*

RB: *They did it with rock music. I mean, you see the billboards. Before anybody did anything, Elvis did it first.*

WW: *Right.*

RB: *I mean, that gotta be a smack in the face to any person, and not just of color. Just anybody—*

WW: *Yeah.*

RB: *—that was into rock music, you know what I'm saying. I* *mean, come on, Chuck Berry. Elvis just basically, just took his whole style.*

WW: *Right. Now you can understand why Little Richard has always been so—*

RB: *I mean, Little Richard, so, you know, it is what it is and we gotta recognize it. I don't think we could stop it. I think we just need to worry, you know, because . . . supporting each other, because if you look at independent record sales, they are not doing well. Never mind major record sales. Independent record sales aren't doing well. So, we just gotta be more responsible for ourself and once we stamp this kid, once we get behind him, then that's when it all happened. And, see, I don't wanna sound like a hypocrite, but, you know, it's like,* The Source *magazine found him an unsigned hype. Um, they gave him two covers, and I'm gonna be honest. I, you know, I don't get into the covers and I don't get into mic rating, uh, you know, I just, I have my opinions.*

I wonder where hip-hop would be without Eminem. And I question whether he has made the game better for everyone. I know Benzino is clear about it, but again, I have mixed feelings. I see the color lines being blurred every day around the music of hip-hop, and I smile. I see young people from opposite sides of the track—both racially and economically—finding a common bond around hip-hop, and I smile. I think racism is real, and in many ways hip-hop and rap have gone a long way toward exposing how silly racism really is.

But I also understand the need and the necessity of keeping it authentic. Hip-hop, in many ways, is a movement, and the catalyst behind the movement must not be distorted.

RB: *You can best believe if hip-hop was in the sixties, then, you know, Malcolm, he woulda been Pac. At the end of the day that's why Pac was so important. It's like, yeah, you can reap the benefits, we can shake our ass and rock the party, but we gotta keep it real, man. Because, you know, when you sit in front of BET, these kids could be in the projects sitting in front of BET and they looking like everything's right, and if they see me with the gold and everything and the jewels and the diamonds, they think everything's right. And I'm the first to let them know it's not right. I'm still in the struggle too. I'm still trying to sell records. My heart is in records. The Almighty RSO was way before* The Source *magazine was developed.*

WW: *Damn right.*

RB: *So, you know what I'm saying? I been into this game for the love of it, man. From day one. And a lot of people would say, well, Eminem's opened up a lot of doors. Man, naw, we've opened up the doors.*

WW: *Right, right, right, right, right, right.*

RB: *He's shutting 'em.*

WW: *Yeah.*

CHAPTER

5

Negroidian

One of the questions I always ask my guests is "How much did that cost?" I love to find out what entertainers do with their money, how much they paid for their houses or cars or rims or clothes. I love to know what a new artist does with his fat advance check and to find out whether he tricked it out on jewelry—which would be very Negroidian.

I coined *Negroidian* as a way to explain all of the crazy things done in entertainment—particularly in the world of hip-hop—with money and behavior. I originally made it up to describe actions and behaviors that are characteristically black. But Negroidian is beyond race. Negroidian is a culture.

Negroidian is universal. If you get an IRS return and you go and blow the entire check on a necklace or a big screen television instead of investing that money, then you are Negroidian. At least stash most of it away for a rainy day—after all, if you're getting a return check, it's *your* money, it's not free cash or a bonus that the government is giving you. It's the money that you overpaid on your taxes that the government is giving back to you.

By the way, all of that money that the government pays

millions of people back in returns, you had better believe they have been collecting interest on that money over the year. So why go and blow it as if it's free money? That's money you worked for that the government has benefited from. Why not go ahead and make that money work for you?

But we live in a Negroidian society. No one thinks like that. For most of us, "extra" money burns a hole in our pockets; we *have* to spend it. Now, *how* we spend it will determine how Negroidian we are. A rapper who gets an advance check for three hundred thousand dollars and blows the whole thing on a new Benz is super Negroidian.

Negroidian behavior is not all negative. There are times when I look at Negroidian acts and I pump my fist and cheer. Some people can be perfectly Negroidian and get away with it. Kimora Simmons having three Bentleys is very Negroidian. But Kimora Simmons can afford to have three Bentleys and not worry about the mortgage not being paid or her children's school tuition getting behind. So, while I may call her Negroidian, I say it with a chuckle and a "You go!"

R & B singer Blu Cantrell, however, talking about spending seventeen thousand dollars a month on her lapdog is very Negroidian, and I mean that in every negative sense. Blu Cantrell bought her little dog a diamond collar and a whole host of Louis Vuitton accessories, as well as satin sheets and all kinds of other doggie items. Now, I understand people loving their dogs and all like that, but Blu Cantrell is one of those artists who needs to save every penny they get. Spending thousands on a dog when you're not certain that you will get that next check from your label is very Negroidian. And dumb!

But the most Negroidian person I have ever interviewed has to be Baby from Cash Money Millionaires. He has a chinchilla bedspread in his bedroom and forty cars—very Negroidian. He walks around with thirty thousand dollars in cash in his possession instead of collecting interest in a money market account—very Negroidian. And while he can afford to do this, is this the smartest thing to do with thirty thousand dollars? Buying forty cars, is that the smartest use of money? Does he really need a chinchilla bedspread?

Baby: But you got some people could do it and some people can't do it. Some people can afford it—

WW: That's true.

Baby: —and some people get put in jams.

WW: Yeah.

Baby: I'm one of them cats that can afford it. I can live my life how I want to.

WW: Yeah. Damn sure can.

Baby: Believe that.

WW: So, do you have houses on both coasts? Do you have an apartment here in New York?

Baby: Nah. I'm planning on getting me one, 'cause I'mma move my office up there by Universal. But I got one in Miami, one in Atlanta, one, New Orleans. I'm kinda cool, but I gotta get me a spot up here.

WW: Yeah. Let me see what all you're wearing on your wrists. Uh, what is that?

Baby: You know.

WW: Okay. Yeah, you're crazy, crazy with it. What kind of watch is this?

Baby: This a Iceman watch, you know what I'm saying?

WW: Iceman watch.

Baby: Yeah

WW: *It's very nice.*

Baby: *Iceman watch with a Jacob piece with a Jacob bracelet with some Jacob earrings.*

WW: *I have to tell you something. Your watch is very understated.*

Baby: *Excuse me.*

WW: *For, it's understated for you. Like I, you know—*

Baby: *I mean it's a everyday piece. If you clown, you catch a . . . I mean, this everyday. Fifteen for everyday, Ma. I mean, how many people could rock a hundred and fifty, two hundred G's on a everyday basis?*

WW: *What is that?*

Baby: *That's some of people houses.*

WW: *Yes. You have two hundred thousand dollars' worth of jewelry on. Period.*

Baby: *And I do at least half a million every time I come out. But I kept it kinda low.*

WW: *Geeze. Donatella Versace's got this thing where she says no less than fifty thousand—excuse me, no less than fifty carats every time she leaves the house. You know whether it's all earrings or—*

Baby: *Yeah, she a bad bitch.*

When Baby, aka Birdman, came to the studio for an interview in 2003, I ran his pockets—made him empty them right there. And he had thousands in cash and a check and a couple hundred thousand dollars' worth of jewelry.

WW: *How much money did you put up there on the table?*

Baby: *I came with like fifty. I was just trying to buy the bar. I was having fun.*

ır pockets right now? Can you

a check.

ets. And don't leave anything in
; not a thing that you can do right
ıs. And he's turning his back as if
still wealthy.

ing there . . .

ney Mack

h me. I got at least thirty cash

I have a counting machine here.
ır stack. How much money is this
ı! This is still in the band from the
hundred. How much money is this

n Avenue.

ı be a forty piece.
u fifty.

nd dollars
hand it's
w against
had not a
American
That's not
other way
here with
l stand in
eir check.
ı this day
and there
thousand
edit card.

you this right now, everybody. I'm
d dollars and it's stacking up three
f one hundred dollar—
me put you up on some game.

than a Whopper, but high as a Big

going shopping. How much you need?
per but high as a Big Mac.

enties laying in your pocket like these

er just gave me them.

WW: *This is your brother?*

Baby: *Nah, Sugar Slim. He ain't make it.*

WW: *Hi, Sugar Slim. Now, what else is in . . . here'*

Baby: *Yeah.*

WW: *Can I see how much this check is for?*

Baby: *That's a little lightweight.*

WW: *I just pulled a check out of his pocket, it was sit* *$66,666.67! Paid to the order of you, N* *Music?!*

Baby: *Yeah.*

WW: *That's you?!*

Baby: *That's part of me.*

WW: *DDB Worldwide Communications on Madisc*

Baby: *She disgusted with it, too, huh?*

WW: *Let's see what else is in your pocket.*

Baby: *I'm good. You drained me, baby girl.*

Walking around with more than a hundred thous
in your pocket. Now, that's real Negroidian! On on
very comical. On the other hand, there ought to be a l
it. I have no problem with him having money, but he
single credit card in his pockets or wallet. Not even an
Express black card, not even a platinum or gold card.
just Negroidian, that's plain old niggerish. There is no
I could put it. And it's very stereotypical. It's right up
people who only use money orders to pay their bills ar
line every two weeks at a check cashing joint to cash t
There is no excuse for not having a checking account i
and age, with all of the banks offering free checking.
is no damn excuse for walking around with a hundred
dollars in your pocket and not have a single charge or c

That's the rich man's version of money orders and check cashing. And it's just niggerish.

While I enjoyed my interview with Baby, running his pockets and finding all of that cash was disappointing. There is no possibility of my being envious of that kind of lifestyle. And I am no way near as wealthy as Baby. As a taxpaying American citizen, there is no part of me that applauds or appreciates the way he handles his money. It's nothing to be proud of. On a scale of one to ten, with ten being the saddest, that's a ten.

And of course, as I talk about him and talked with him, I saw his home celebrated on *MTV Cribs*. I saw some of the forty whips, I saw the sixty-thousand-dollar chinchilla throw on his bed. On some level I can appreciate that. Anyone with a chinchilla bedspread has mad money. But to see it walking and talking in a pocket was another thing.

We can thank *MTV Cribs* for taking Negroidian behavior to an all-time high. It has put that mentality on display for all to see and all to compete with. From Master P's gold ceilings in his mansion and the custom-made, tricked-out, Gucci-interior Mercedes that he purchased for his son, Lil Romeo, who wasn't even old enough to drive, to Missy Elliot's Lamborghini bed that cost something like $100,000. Just Negroidian. And then there was Sisqo (whatever happened to him?) with his house with the huge basketball court out back. I would love to see a follow-up on *Cribs* to see who still has their homes and who was fronting all along. It's very Negroidian to front—to act like you have everything and really have nothing. To drive a Bentley and rent a house or an apartment is Negroidian.

I can appreciate the hustle and all of the posturing people do to have the look of luxury, to appear to have all of the trappings of success. You cannot be a platinum-selling artist and not have certain things, at least that's what the game says. So you do what you have to do—even if you don't have it.

I never used to think that way, but as I get deeper in this game myself, I realize the importance of having the trappings and all of the so-called tools of the trade. As I look at myself, I must admit that I, too, am prone to Negroidian behavior. But I thank my husband for that. He brought the Negroid out in me. Kevin is from Brownsville, Brooklyn. He comes from the streets, and as a self-made man he has a unique perspective on the game that we're in and the expectations that accompany it. He offers me interesting insight into things that I would not normally think about myself because I was not brought up to look at Negroidian expenditures as being something of substance.

Prior to meeting my husband, my Pathfinder was fine. I had investment property in Florida and I had a little money in the bank. But when I met my husband, within the first eight months of dating, out went the Pathfinder, replaced by a sporty new Benz, and within minutes of that we got a Range Rover to add to the collection.

Yes, I have three Birkin bags. Three. That's very Negroidian, and it's a little embarrassing to admit. But I do have an explanation. When I wanted to get one, there was a huge waiting list, especially after *Sex and the City* made it very popular. Actually, *Sex and the City* was responsible for women getting their bag game together. And bags are my weakness. I put my name on the list. It took three years for my name to come up, and I got my bag. It was black. Ugh! Birkin bags come in so many beautiful colors, and I would have wanted any color but black. But after a wait like that, I took what they gave me.

Shortly after this, I knew someone who was going to Paris, and I asked them to stop in Hermès and pick me up a Birkin bag

This is me in my senior year at Ocean Township High School. This is the girl who I am today. All the shit I've been through and survived, when I look at this picture, I know that I have now come full circle, right back to her. This is who I am inside right now.

I knew I would be a star. I would have my sister, Wanda, take Polaroid pictures of me and I would give them out and autograph them when I did an appearance for my college station. This is one of the pictures.

This is me in 1987. I'd just graduated from college and I was in St. Croix to start my first radio job at WVIS. I'm wearing what my father calls my "garbage bag outfit" to hide my weight.

Who *are* these people? I have no idea. But look at me faking it, acting like they are my best friends and we are having lots of fun. Schmooze your way to the top, I say!

Me and Mo'Nique from *The Parkers* and *It's Showtime at the Apollo*. We were actually teamed up to do a television show together in the 1990s. Today we don't speak. She started calling me a drag queen in her comedy routine and, well, I decided to finish it on the *Wendy Williams Experience* every chance I got. Judging from this picture, Mo'nique is not really happy being fat. I know I wasn't, so I decided to do something about it.

I hate photo shoots, and this is why. These clothes didn't fit. In fact, the pants aren't even buttoned in the back. I hated my body. But again, you have to fake it until you make it!

Me and Janet Jackson. I didn't realize how tiny she is. And look at my body language. I feel like a giant monster next to her. I'm not showing any teeth (which is rare). I'm feeling really bad about myself standing next to Janet Jackson. Shortly after this picture I decided to get plastic surgery.

Me and Steve Manning. Steve is a publicist extraordinaire! He can be found anywhere there are fabulous people, like at the Jackson compound on Thanksgiving. By the way, he is my Jackson family insider.

Where are they now III? Big Lez and Tracey Lee. She was everywhere at one point, dancing in videos and even hosting a show on BET. And Tracey Lee was supposed to be the next rap sensation In this game you'd better make the most of your fifteen minutes because they are gone quickly.

Me and Skelytor, my first assistant and engineer. We sure went through a lot together. Shout out to you, Skelytor!

Missy Elliott and Yo-Yo. That's Missy at her heaviest, sporting a crunchy pineapple on her head.

This is Lil' Kim in an impromptu performance at the Dons & Divas Extravaganza 2003. I love Kim, but she has gone too far with the plastic surgery (yes, look who's talking).

Me and Queen Pen. By the way, where is she now? You had better not say one word, because from the looks of this picture, Queen Pen will fuck you up! In fact, she will fuck you up for the both of us!

Me and Flava Flav from Public Enemy. He came to my station in Philly and didn't know I was there and wasn't expecting a real interview. When I started asking him about substance abuse, he got mad and called my mother a crackhead. I called him a bum and he walked out. They got him back to take this picture. He's still mad. And as you can see, I am not amused.

Me and the Wu-Tang Clan in an ad for MacWear, which I used to endorse. Clearly you could tell from the cuts in Method Man's beard that he was destined for break-out stardom. And clearly you could tell from the way Ol' Dirty Bastard is hiding in the photo that he was destined for craziness.

Me and Cam'ron. This is Cam'ron when he had some weight and me at my skinniest. I later found out that my dramatic weight loss was due to a thyroid condition. I contemplated letting it go to stay that thin. And now there are rumors about Cam'ron and his weight loss.

This is Pras and Wyclef of the Fugees. Where is Lauryn Hill? Who knows. She flaked out a long time ago.

Lisa Raye, Mekhi Phifer and me at the Dons & Divas Extravaganza 2003. Lisa Raye and Mekhi hosted the star-studded bash that included Lil' Kim, Jaheim, and Mayor Sharpe James from Newark among the dignitaries.

Me and Tyson Beckford and my morning team, Tony Richards (red hat), and Dee Lee. Tyson spent the entire interview with his back to me, facing the wall. You can tell from my expression that we have issues.

Speaking of issues . . . this is me and R. Kelly. I used to be one of his biggest fans. But now I want to throw up every time I see him.

Me and my parents. This is one of my proudest moments. We're at a very "susie" affair to celebrate the success of my bestselling book, *Wendy's Got the Heat*. This is one of the first times my parents got to see the other side of what I do, complete with paparazzi. This was a fun evening!

in blue. So I shelled out another six thousand dollars for that bag. (Oh, yeah, they cost six thousand dollars.) And then I had to get a red one because I love the color. So I have three and they are my most prized possessions. I use one of my Birkin bags five times a week. Ironically, the black one is the one I use more than any of them. They still captivate me. I don't consider them really Negroidian, I planned and plotted for each one and I wanted them. And I like that you can't just pick up a knockoff Birkin bag on Canal Street in New York, where you can get every other kind of knockoff. I have to be current.

What Kevin taught me was that in our line of work, people enjoy doing business with people who have the tools of the trade. If someone is going to meet you and you are someone in the public eye, they really don't want to see you drive up in a sensible car. It's terribly interesting. And terribly Negroidian. People don't want to see you wearing a sensible wool coat in the winter. They want to see you fluffed out in a chinchilla or a mink.

And they don't want to see you with sensible gold balls in your ears, they want to see you dripping in diamonds. And your hair had better be done, freshly dipped. Your jeans had better be down and your shoes had better not be turned over. You may have on work boots, (and I believe that work boots should be to work in and have some mud on them), but when you're a celebrity they better be clean. Especially when you're a *black* celebrity. There is a lot of pressure on black celebrities. And I totally understand it.

I used to drive a Subaru when I got out of college. And one of my first radio jobs was at HOT when it was HOT-103. I was very popular on the station, because I did many appearances and had a little bit of celebrity within the pop community. I remember pulling up to a 7-Eleven to get a pack of cigarettes one day and some listeners pulled up next to me. The girl was driving a brand-new cabriolet and she had a couple of friends with her. The crew looked like they were having so much fun—Barbie and Ken and Midge. It was a nice summer day and they were chilling in the bright white cabriolet with the top down. And there I was in my dirty brown Subaru with no air conditioning, windows down, looking sweaty.

As I was getting out, I heard one of them say, "Wow, we have a better car than *her*!" They knew I was Wendy from the radio, and I guess they hadn't expected me to have a car like that. The comment stung a little. But it wasn't delivered with any malice, just matter of fact. And I understood their surprise.

But the sting would have been magnified had I pulled up next to a car full of black people. I would have gotten hit in a very Negroidian way with "You see that car!" It would have been so loud and nasty, I would have wanted to crawl under my car. And that kind of attitude seems only directed at black people by black people. I cannot imagine a black person opening her mouth to say, "That's all they're driving?!" directed at a white celebrity.

White celebrities get a free pass. It's a serious double standard. If you're pulling up at a traffic light and you look over and the guy in the next car is from the band Blink 182 and he's driving a beat-down Chevy, no one is looking at him like "Ewww, look at that!" The assumption is that he has money because he's in Blink 182. They would think, "That's just a crazy white boy with that grunge thing." We don't make fun of his uncombed hair, his beat-down jeans, his turned-over shoes. We still assume he has money. We think that he probably has mad houses or farms or whatever white boys like that live in.

But black celebrities are forced to get tools of the trade, and I hate it. It's really silly. But it's a reality.

I have found that the very people who are pointing and saying, "I have a better car!" are the same people who have nothing *but* that car.

The Negroidian thing goes way beyond celebrity. I attribute a lot of the behavior to not being used to having money. For many black people, our money is all brand-new. Generally speaking, a lot of us are second-generation college graduates. A lot of us are first-generation college graduates. Very few of us are third- and fourth-generation college graduates. Hardly any of us were born into family businesses with a silver spoon in our mouths. Right now, we are probably striving as much as we have ever been as far as having things and money and raising our children into a certain lifestyle.

Look at the way Kimora and Russell Simmons's children are being raised—in multimillionaire neighborhoods with nannies, the best education, with a certain class and etiquette, a knowledge of all of the finest things in life, not wanting for a thing. The same for the children of Will and Jada. And Puffy's kids. They may never be touched by the ills of the streets.

But there are also many noncelebrities hustling to provide a different reality for their family. There are households where Mommy and Daddy both went to college. Mommy is a Ph.D. and daddy is a chemist and they have a nice house. Or both Mommy and Daddy work very hard and are sending their children to private school and are struggling to have the nice things—but they have *all* of the nice things.

I look at some of the things my son has and how he's being raised, and I am in awe over what we are able to give our children now . . . some of us. But with the toys, games, and electronics, we are also missing some very important values . . . some of us. Too many of us are putting our entire worth into those things, which is Negroidian in the negative. We are raising our children to value things and possessions instead of values like love, integrity, and morality. They want all of the latest things, and parents are literally breaking their bank to give it to them. I think this is wrong. And the stakes seem to be higher today than ever before. Kids don't want Air Force Ones, they want Prada sneakers. They don't want the Murakami (the rainbow colors) anymore. It's too common. They want the Louis Vuitton Theda bag. These kids want it all. And parents have to learn how to say no.

But how can they when many parents are worse than the kids? They want the Manolo Blahniks and the Jimmy Choo—not the Payless knockoffs (they don't care what Star Jones is talking about).

Too many look down their noses at people for not having things instead of being grateful for what they do have. We shouldn't be at a point where we can afford to pull up to one another and sniff our noses and say, "Hmm, that's all you're driving!"

I have an old soul's opinion about material things, and while I talk about materialistic things a lot on my show, in real life I am still that frugal person who clips coupons and has occasional flashbacks to the elderly lady who is so poor that she has to eat cat food. I never want that to be me, so while I have the "tools of the trade" and all of the trappings of a celebrity lifestyle, I still stash money and am very careful about cutting into my retirement fund or my son's education fund. I will do without before ever doing that.

And in the midst of what appears to be Negroidian behavior on my part, when you see me out with a pink fur and matching pink fur hat or the crazy jewelry that I may have on, know that in my personal life, at the end of the day, none of those things matter to me one bit. I recognize that without someone significant in your life, no material thing matters. Life is so much bigger than that.

If your kids are in remedial reading or your baby's mom is giving you drama, who cares how much money you have or how many cars are in your driveway? When you are lonely, no Cartier bracelet or Louis bag is going to fill that hole.

Things do help, but they aren't the end-all. I know it feels good to pull out of that mile-long driveway in a nice whip but if your household is a mess, what does it all matter?

CHAPTER
6
Puff, Puff, Pass

This will be the shortest chapter in this book because I really don't have much to say on the subject, and after I have said what I am going to say, I want to put this whole issue to rest—once and for all.

For the record, I do not hate Sean "Puff Daddy, Puffy, P. Diddy" Combs. I do not hate anyone, for that matter. I do, however, hold a certain level of contempt for Puffy. He single-handedly tried to ruin me, tried to ruin my career. He spent a lot of money and used a lot of his influence to try to crush me in New York in the late 1990s. Much of this is part of a sealed court record in a suit filed by me against my former station at HOT-97, and some of it was covered in *Wendy's Got the Heat.* It's old news, and I don't really want to rehash the gory details, but I will say that Puffy almost accomplished his goal. And the hell he put me through, I will never forget. But I don't hate him.

Puffy is in a special category with me. I will call it "other"— as in other than everyone else.

I recently went on a rant on the *Experience* where I had some harsh words for Puffy. Much of it was for dramatic effect for the radio. And some may pick up this book and see exclusive interviews with people directly connected to Puffy and think that this is my way of getting him back. Well, it isn't.

Let's be honest, Puffy is the biggest name in hip-hop—from the music, to the clothes, to the legend. Many of the things that hip-hop is today, it owes to Puffy. And being the biggest name in hip-hop also makes him the biggest target for scandality. People want to talk about him, and you people want to know what people are saying.

Perhaps the real reason why there are so many references to Puffy in this book is because of Puffy himself.

I didn't build the aura that he has around him. I didn't create the scene at City College where nine people lost their lives in 1991 at a charity event run by him. I didn't have Puffy smack in the middle of a murder of his Bad Boy artist Christopher "Biggie" Wallace in Los Angeles in 1997.

I wasn't there at Club New York in 1999 when shots rang out and a police chase ensued. I wasn't on trial for attempted murder and I didn't cause the events that led to the conviction of Bad Boy artist Jamal "Shyne" Barrow, who was sentenced to ten years in prison.

I didn't have anything to do with Bad Boy artist Mason "Ma$e" Betha leaving the business, fearing for his life. And I wasn't there in 2004 when Bad Boy artist Loon was arrested and charged with attempted murder for a stabbing outside of a Los Angeles nightclub. And I certainly didn't have anything to do with Puffy shirking his responsibilities and not ponying up enough child support to adequately take care of his firstborn child.

There seems to be this black cloud over Puffy. Call it karma, call it kismet, call it what you want. I didn't create it, but I damn sure will talk about it.

So forget about whatever he did to me. I will not go into details about that. Just know that Puffy has given me and all of the wags plenty of grist for our mills. If he doesn't like what's written about him, he has only himself to blame.

Puffy is a person who stays in the news. That is one thing he has done for my career—giving me much to talk about. And I love him for that. If it's not Diddy Running the City for the children, he's paying off Wardell Fenderson, the driver of the getaway car from Club New York. Or he's renting a yacht for four hundred thousand dollars a day with fabulous celebrities aboard. Or he's bedding some hot star. Or starring on Broadway.

I don't hate. I thank. I even buy my son Sean John outfits. I love his clothing line. I appreciate Puffy. I even look forward one day to sitting down with him for a little chat. The last time I interviewed Puffy was around 1991 before the City College incident. It was a great time in the studio, lots of fun and laughs. We talked about his big event. I was even supposed to be on the sidelines for that celebrity/charity basketball game as a cheerleader. It was a regular interview—but definitely not an *Experience* interview. I wasn't Wendy the way I am now and he wasn't the Puffy that he is now.

The last time I saw him was at a play in Manhattan in the winter of 2004. It was at the opening of *Women Can't Wait,* the one-woman play by Sarah Jones. Sarah Jessica Parker was there and Puffy sat in front of me a couple of rows down. He came in as the play was to begin. He saw me. And I saw him. He didn't acknowledge me.

The only kind of acknowledgment that I would accept would be "I'm coming by to see you on your show."

I would love to interview Puffy. But it isn't a goal of mine. I set reasonable goals for myself—goals that I have some assuredness that I can make happen. Interviewing Puffy isn't very reasonable because it doesn't depend solely upon me. So if it happens, great.

What would I ask him? He would have to find out when he comes into the studio. But I can say that I will not be asking him, "Are you gay?" We're way beyond that.

CHAPTER

7

A Wendy Williams Exclusive
Wardell Fenderson, the Driver

December 27, 1999, is a date that is permanently etched in the mind of Wardell Fenderson. That was the day his life was to change forever. As a driver for Sean "Puffy, P. Diddy, Whatever He Is Calling Himself These Days" Combs, Wardell Fenderson was asked to drive Puffy and his then-girlfriend, Jennifer Lopez, to Club New York, where they planned on partying the night away—a post-Christmas, pre–New Year's celebration that would turn into a disaster for all involved.

It was a routine assignment for Wardell that went very, very bad when shots rang out and all hell broke loose inside the club. In the middle of the melee was his client—Puffy.

Wardell, who was filling in as Puffy's driver as a favor to a friend, had been driving the rap mogul for just a few weeks when this incident happened. And when he pulled up to Club New York's entrance as he was instructed, Puffy and his entourage (minus Jennifer at first) piled into the SUV and ordered Wardell to drive. According to Wardell, one of the bodyguards had to go back in—Wardell contends that Puffy had totally forgotten about the love of his life at the time—Jennifer.

J.Lo finally emerged from the club and Wardell said he had no idea what had really happened inside until J.Lo blurted out, "Shyne busted off! Shyne busted off!" Police arrived at the scene, and according to Wardell and his trial testimony, he was ordered by Puffy and his bodyguard Anthony "Wolf" Jones to drive and "keep driving!" And he did.

Eleven red lights later, Wardell finally pulled over, was arrested for the first time in his life, according to him, and that's when he says his personal nightmare began. A gun was found in the car. Another was found near the scene. And while in jail, Wardell said he was offered a bribe from Puffy—a twenty-five-thousand-dollar ring—to take the rap for the gun found in the car. He even testified to that before a grand jury. Puffy said that if Wardell agreed to claim the gun was his, he and his family would be taken care of. Out of fear, Wardell initially said he would take the rap. But he said he quickly came to his senses when he was released (Puffy had him bailed out of jail) and realized what he was facing. He didn't take Puffy's ring and didn't take the rap.

A taped phone conversation had Puffy offering to make Wardell—who had lost his real job driving for an investment banker amid the negative publicity following the club shooting—and his family "comfortable," according to court documents. Wardell testified against Puffy.

On March 16, 2001, after a two-month trial, Puffy—who was defended by all-star attorneys Johnnie Cochran and Benjamin Brafman—was cleared of weapons possession and bribery charges. His codefendant and bodyguard, Anthony "Wolf" Jones, was also acquitted of all charges. But Puffy's protégé, Jamal "Shyne" Barrow, who had a separate defense team, was found guilty of assault and weapons charges and was sentenced to ten years in prison. He is still in prison. (Wolf was shot to death at Chaos, an Atlanta nightclub, in November 2003, allegedly in an argument over a woman.)

In many ways, it looked as though Wardell Fenderson was also a loser in the case. The jury obviously didn't find his sworn testimony credible enough to convict Puffy of bribery. And after meeting Wardell, I somewhat understand. It's not the things that Wardell says. He's just a quirky little dude. He had some very interesting things to say, but I could see why the jury in the first trial did not find him credible. And it didn't help that Puffy's lawyer Benjamin Brafman painted Wardell as a liar and a deadbeat dad.

"You have to look at who the person is saying it," said Brafman to the jury. "What do you know about Wardell Fenderson? What type of person abandons, for all practical purposes, the welfare of his own child?" Wardell had confessed to owing about seventy thousand dollars in child support.

I also found Wardell to be very courageous to take on Puffy the way he did. Don't get it twisted. In my opinion, Puffy is a very dangerous man. He may not wear his danger the way someone like, say, Suge Knight—who is six four, and 350 pounds—wears his, but he is dangerous all the same. Suge wears his fear and intimidation, Puffy hides his behind shiny suits, which makes him more dangerous because you don't necessarily see him coming.

Something is rotten in Puffy's camp. I am still baffled how he was able to walk away scot-free while Shyne got ten years. I think he sold his soul to the devil a long time ago, to be quite honest with you. Perhaps that's why things like this keep happening to Puffy. And credit to Wardell for having enough balls to not back down.

Wardell Fenderson used to call me on the request line on WBLS after I returned to New York in 2001. I was still in Philly when the mess jumped off at Club New York, but when I got back to New York he called me to welcome me back and he would call me frequently on the request line. I would never put him on blast and I never put his calls on the air. I would shout him out here and there.

He had been calling to chat. But I knew he was open to me asking him questions. A person doesn't call so many times on a request line without a reason. He wanted exposure and he wanted to tell his story and perhaps get a little bit of celebrity. Because celebrity is like a drug.

I decided to keep Wardell as a feather in my cap for a one-on-one interview, whether in the studio or, as it turned out, for this book. I kept his number handy and at the right time, I used it.

I interviewed Wardell Fenderson on November 10, 2003, at a special meeting spot in Manhattan. He was wearing glasses and a gray Kangol and said he was very tired. Since the 1999 Club New York incident, Wardell, whose nickname is Woody, has had to take lesser jobs than he was accustomed to and was working crazy hours to make ends meet.

We talked for more than an hour about everything from how he started working for Puffy to how Puffy treated J.Lo to what really jumped off that night at Club New York. He was very soft-spoken and answered every question without hesitation. He seemed relieved to finally get it all off his chest. As it turned out, it was the last interview he was to do before his big trial. And as it turned out, it may be the last interview he will ever get to do on the subject.

Since our talk, Wardell has done quite well for himself. After more than a year of trying, he was able to finally serve Jennifer

Lopez—who had proven to be quite elusive—with papers to testify at his civil trial. He had someone set up to act like they wanted her autograph. When she took the paper to sign, she was officially served.

It was brilliant because serving J.Lo may have been the very thing to settle his case. In addition to not wanting to testify himself, perhaps Puffy in an act of gallantry settled the case rather than put J.Lo through the whole rigmarole of a trial.

On February 3, 2004, Wardell, forty-five, who was suing Puffy for three million dollars for emotional suffering, loss of work, and false imprisonment, had his case settled by Puffy for an undisclosed amount that I have been told is somewhere in the neighborhood of $1.2 million. Not bad, Wardell. Not bad at all.

I originally thought Wardell should have taken the ring and the money that Puffy allegedly offered him. But I guess he knew better. I thought he would end up with nothing . . . but a story to tell.

He ended up with money *and* a story to tell.

INTERVIEW SESSION
Wardell Fenderson

WW: This is Wardell Fenderson. Wardell Fenderson, everybody!
        The interesting part of meeting you are the interesting sto-
        ries, of things making sense about J.Lo and Puffy. So how
        long have you been driving?

WF: As a professional?

WW: Yes.

WF: Since 1979.

WW: You have driven some famous people.

WF: Very famous.

WW: Like who?

WF: Robert De Niro, Bill Murray, Harrison Ford. I worked for a
        limousine service, and these were some of the people that
        I happen to come across. I've even driven the late great
        Leonard Bernstein.

WW: These are one-time drives?

WF: Some. You never knew who you would be driving.

WW: What was the longest celebrity contract you had?

WF: Actually, working for Puffy for those three months.

WW: How did you come to know Puffy to drive for him those
        three months?

WF: A friend of mine, who was Puffy's weekend driver for more
        than a year, was going into the hospital to have surgery.
        And he asked me to hold the job down for him. I arranged
        with my boss to have my weekends free to do it. And that's
        how it happened.

WW: Were you excited?

WF: At first I was excited. Then I started seeing the shenani-
        gans and I knew the job would be more than I bargained

for. Coming from a corporate environment and driving mostly wealthy corporate executives, CEOs, and company owners and going into this was like a culture shock.

WW: So would Puff and Jennifer [Lopez] ever have sex in the cars?

WF: I wouldn't know anything about that. I have never witnessed that.

WW: What did you mostly drive? Suburbans?

WF: A Navigator and his Bentley.

WW: I always say it's very hot to be seen in a Suburban or a Yukon, with the windows blacked out, but you lose your privacy as a celebrity. If you pull up in a stretch, it's not trendy at all. It's corny.

So, was he open with you—as far as his phone conversations or conversations with others in the car? Or was it guarded conversation?

WF: He was always on the phone, talking with someone. Sometimes he was talking in hushed tones.

WW: See, I would be a nervous wreck because there you are in the car.

WF: I was invisible—

WW: —until something jumps off. Can you lead us up to the time—that terrible night at Club New York? Had you taken he and Jennifer out?

WF: Most of the time when I drove him or her, it was never to any private planes or anything. It was usually to or from a video shoot.

WW: Were they lovey-dovey in the car?

WF: Not much. But they did have their moments.

WW: Did you ever witness them fight?

WF: Yes.

WW: Is she strong, like fearless?

WF: Not at all. He would belittle her and sometimes have her on the verge of tears, which would put me in an uncomfortable position. It wouldn't happen all the time. But when it did—

WW: Would it ever be just you and her?

WF: No, there was a bodyguard present all the time.

WW: Was Puffy's persona with the bodyguard that of a friend, a comrade, one of being protected, or that of employer-employee?

WF: It all varied, depending on Puffy's mood.

WW: His mood controlled everything? Did his mood control Jennifer?

WF: I would say so. She knew who was in charge of that relationship. . . .

WW: And it was him.

WF: Oh, yeah!

WW: Wow! The image that a lot of people have of Jennifer Lopez is as this strong, fearless woman. I happen to believe that she has a soft and pink side, the side you're talking about. Soft and pink behavior. So I'm not shocked. But I know people might be shocked to hear that. Is Puffy a nice boss?

WF: I never saw him as being a nice person. He is controlling, very arrogant, and feeling like "My money can take me anywhere."

WW: Would he call Jennifer a dumb bitch?

WF: I had not heard that. But he has a temper. I have heard him use obscenities toward her.

WW: Janice Combs. Have you ever driven her?

WF: One of the first times I drove him, I drove her too.

WW: Was she a nice woman?

WF: She was happy because she finally had somebody decent with a little bit of class [driving]. I talked with her about my family, about my vacation, as opposed to women and things like that.

WW: Did Puffy hang out with a lot of male friends?

WF: Him and Shyne used to hang out a lot.

WW: Did he come to his house a lot?

WF: Shyne was basically under his wing a lot. That's why, quite frankly, I was shocked by the way it all went down. Maybe when Shyne comes out [of jail] there will be twenty million dollars waiting for him. I don't know. You never know. Smoke and mirrors.

WW: How did Jennifer get along with Shyne? Puffy and Shyne were like Matt Damon and Ben Affleck. They were working on music together. How did Jennifer act around Shyne?

WF: I didn't pay any attention. I didn't notice any way she treated him or anyone else. I drove Puffy most of the time without Jennifer, like to the Video Music Awards. Most of the time I drove, it was just him. Two out of three times it was just him with a bodyguard.

WW: Have you ever driven Kim Porter, Puffy's baby's mother?

WF: I did drive her occasionally.

WW: Was she a nice woman?

WF: I stayed in my place as a chauffeur.

WW: Did she tip well?

WF: I never got a tip.

WW: Was Puffy cheap?

WF: It depends on who he is spending the money on. I never got a dime extra from him. I never got a grape. I got what I was making, but never nothing extra.

WW: Was he with Bentley Farnsworth at that time?

WF: No.

WW: Let's talk about that night at Club New York. What time did you meet up with Puffy?

WF: I cannot remember the exact time. It was somewhere around eleven. I met him at the parking lot across from his studio [Daddy's House], a block away from the club.

WW: How did he get to the studio?

WF: I picked him up from the Hamptons.

WW: How did Jennifer get there?

WF: She came from the Hamptons with him. His mother was out there too.

WW: So he's there and asks you to pick him up. And you drive him and Jennifer to the club. So you get to the club and what happens?

WF: There are a whole lot of people there. It's a real scene.

WW: I imagine, after the incident popped off in the club, the doors bursting open and Puffy and Jennifer come running out, her hair flying, getting caught in the door as it closes. You didn't go in the club, right?

WF: I have no idea what happened in the club. I got a call to meet them in front of the club. "Make sure you're ready to come out, because the police are not going to let me sit on the street, and if they tell me to move I will have to circle the block and that may take a while, so make sure they're ready to come out," I told the bodyguard. He said, "Okay, I'll call you back." About ten minutes later he called me back and said, "We're heading for the door now."

        So I pulled the Navigator right outside the door when all of a sudden I see people come diving out of the club screaming, "They're shooting, they're shooting!"

WW: You are ly-ing!

WF: I put the car in gear and I was ready to peel out.

WW: You were ready to leave Puffy and Jennifer there?!

WF: I would have left. I wasn't waiting around to see anything metal coming my way.

WW: You have a wife, you have kids?

WF: I have a family. I have three kids.

WW: In other words, you have something to get off the block for. You have something to live for.

WF: Exactly.

WW: Wow! So, through the melee, you see Puffy and Jennifer? Or do you see the bodyguards? Who do you see first?

WF: Puffy comes out with Curtis, one of his bodyguards. Jennifer is nowhere in sight.

WW: What?!

WF: The car door opens and Curtis is trying to get Puffy in the car. But Puffy, in a moment of gallantry, says, "No, we can't leave without Jennifer!" So Curtis goes back inside to retrieve Jennifer. And Jennifer comes out of another door with Wolf.

WW: So where's Curtis?

WF: He's back in the club looking for Jennifer, but she already came out of another door. She gets in the backseat with Puffy. Wolf gets in the front seat, in front of Puffy. And Jennifer is seated behind me.

WW: I imagine Puffy sitting in the back, screaming like a bitch. You say what?

WF: He's saying, "Yo, dog, how do you open the stash! Open the stash!"

WW: Is his voice like twenty octaves high when he was talking?

WF: Yeah. He was a nervous wreck.

WW: Is this his truck?

WF: It is registered to Bad Boy.

WW: In other words, this is his truck and he's asking you how to open the stash?

WF: Which I never even knew existed.

WW: Of course! Who is thinking that? What about Wolf—what is he doing?

WF: He's asking the same question.

WW: And he's screaming too?

WF: Yes. And Jennifer was screaming, "Shyne busted off in the air! Shyne busted off in the air!"

WW: Is she crying? Is she talking like a ghetto princess?

WF: It was like a scene out of a movie. We should have had cameras in the car.

WW: Who was the biggest bitch in the car?

WF: Puffy was.

WW: Well, I guess he had the most to lose. So Jen is screaming. And does Puffy turn to her in a moment of stress and say, "Shut the fuck up, bitch?!"

WF: No. He is too busy constantly asking me to open the stash and telling me to drive.

WW: So you pass one light, two lights, three lights, ten fucking lights, eleven lights. You must have been driving . . . how fast?

WF: We weren't going that fast. We just weren't stopping. It wasn't a high-speed chase. I would come to a red light and I would check the cross traffic before going through. I wasn't just barreling out of control through the lights. I was concerned about my safety.

WW: Was one of the things going through your mind, "I am quitting this job in the morning"?

WF: Ironically, that was supposed to be my last night driving him. After I dropped off his mother from the Hamptons, I asked him if he would be needing me. He said, "No, I'm not coming back until Monday or Tuesday." And I only drove on the weekends. So this was going to be my last night driving him. I was going to go to Bad Boy offices that Monday and let them know that I would no longer be driving for them.

WW: Oh, my God! That's amazing. So, Wardell, how much were you making, if you don't mind me asking?

WF: Two hundred and fifty dollars a day. No matter whether I worked two hours or fifteen hours. It was the same.

WW: So that's five hundred dollars for the weekend. . . . So at the eleventh light, what is the fever in the car?

WF: Panic, bedlam, frenzy.

WW: Where was the stash? Did you ever open it?

WF: It was explained to me that the stash was somewhere in the console. I never got to see it. It opened a secret compartment in the car. There was some combination that you had to know that included adjusting the temperature, the radio, and pushing some other controls to make it open. The genius didn't know how to open his own stash. A rocket scientist.

WW: So a gun goes flying out of the window at some point.

WF: I never saw the gun. I saw the amber light flood the car. And I know he put his window down.

WW: A gun was found on the street by cops.

WF: That's what I heard, and one was found under Wolf's seat.

WW: That was after you guys finally pulled over.

WF: Yeah. And when the cops stopped us and we all got out of the car, Jennifer tried to walk away. The cops said, "Where do you think you're going?" She said, "It's not my gun!" Those were her exact words, and she proceeded to walk down the street.

WW: Was she crying? Or was she Jenny from the block? Tough?

WF: She broke down in the car.

WW: What was her demeanor when the cops stopped you?

WF: I have no idea. I didn't have time to have a demeanor, I was already in handcuffs and in the back of a police car.

WW: What made you pull over after you ran the eleventh light? Did they barricade you?

WF: There was a police car that I would have had to evade and continue the chase. I was really concerned.

WW: Be damned everybody else.

WF: I said, "Okay, guys. Chase over!"

WW: Before the cops had a chance to talk to you, is that when Puffy offered you his ring?

WF: He said he wanted me to hold it as collateral to make sure I knew he was good for the money. But he didn't offer me the ring until we got into the jail.

WW: Did you take the ring?

WF: No.

WW: What's going on in your mind? Is it money, what we all want so much? This is your ticket to a full-time driving job. You got a fifty-thousand-dollar ring. He will match the money and still let you keep the ring? And you would be driving for him permanently probably for about seven hundred dollars a night.

WF: Or I would probably be dead.

WW: Do you go to church?

WF: I go to church occasionally. But I have God in my heart, always.

WW: So they put Jen in cuffs, how did that look?

WF: I didn't see her in cuffs. All I know I was the first one to have a gun pointed at my head. I was the first one out of that vehicle. I was the first one in handcuffs.

WW: Well, you were driving the getaway car. Did they have the gun they found in the street?

WF: That was allegedly found at another time and turned in by someone else—not the cops. That came out during the trial.

WW: When they asked you about it, did you tell them about the open window?

WF: I cooperated with the district attorney.

WW: How did your life change after that night?

WF: I lost a dream job, driving for an executive at a major corporation. This was my regular nine-to-five, so to speak. This was my main gig. And I lost it. I would rather not say the name of the man or the company because he's a very private man but after that fiasco, he called me and said, "Listen, Woody, I really love you."—Woody is my nickname—"I like you working for my family, but I cannot have you driving my family around with the possibility of someone from that club coming after you at any moment. I cannot risk that around my family." And I couldn't blame him. I couldn't blame him.

WW: There's been a lawsuit filed.

WF: Yes, in October 2000.

WW: It's been a long, arduous process. How much are you suing for?

WF: Three million dollars. And they dismissed one of the counts. I don't know how these things work.

WW: What are you suing for?

WF: Unlawful imprisonment and assault, verbal assault.

WW: Is Puffy a verbally abusive man?

WF: To people? Yeah!

WW: To you ever?

WF: No, I wouldn't put up with it. I would have left that job a long time ago, if he were verbally abusive. I don't care who you are, I don't take that.

WW: When do you think you will know something?

WF: In December/January. [Note: The trial started in January. And on February 2, 2004, a day before Sean Combs was to testify at the trial, he settled out of court for an undisclosed amount.]

WW: Do you have posttraumatic stress from that?

WF: They made me feel very uncomfortable.

WW: Did you detect any *How You Doin'?* while working with Puffy?

WF: *Ohhh, How You Doin'?* (Laughter.) One night, I was picking Shyne up from his residence and was taking him to the Peninsula Hotel in Manhattan. Puffy was in the car and he was describing to Shyne an incident where a Caucasian man who didn't recognize his celebrity status had actually made a sexual advance toward him. And from the conversation, I got that Puffy thought it was funny that this guy was coming on to him. He didn't sound like he was offended at all—which is the reaction of most straight men.

WW: Have you ever seen Puffy express feminine characteristics or emotions toward men?

WF: No. The only interaction I had with him was in the car.

WW: Did you ever drop him off at a questionable address, up the street and around the corner, where you knew where he was really going?

For years I have been told about private parties where people looking for a particular service can find what they are looking for. For instance, I work with somebody who is into feet. He goes to exclusive foot fetish parties. The parties are thrown every week and the venue is changed about every two months. It can be in a fabulous brownstone on the Upper East Side or a well-appointed loft on the Lower East Side of Manhattan. The host is well paid. The music is right. The food is perfect. The women are top shelf. And it's by invitation only.

My coworker told me that he enjoys these parties immensely. He tells me that he enjoys washing the perfect feet of these women, and applying lotion and rubbing their feet. It's not about the full-blown sex for him. It's about the feet. And he loves it.

I'm not sure what kind of party or venue Fenderson was dropping Puffy off to, but there are all kinds of secret parties and gathering spots throughout the city. Perhaps the address Wardell Fenderson is referring to was a secret party address.

WF: There was a scandalous address, which I found very strange because he never took any security with him and he would have me wait around the corner.

WW: What's the address?

WF: I cannot give you an exact address. I will say only that it's an Upper East Side address.

WW: Could be innocent.

WF: He would walk back to the car.

WW: How long would you wait?

WF: An hour. Sometimes half an hour, forty minutes—not even enough time to get a decent bite to eat, because I never knew when he would be coming out. We had a designated meeting spot.

WW: Did he seem more at peace after coming out—like he wanted to smoke a cigarette or something?

WF: (*Laughter.*) I've never seen him smoke a cigarette . . .

WW: I was playing . . .

WF: . . . not a legal one, anyway.

WW: Oh! Ding-ding!

WF: Oh, yeah!

WW: Is his name Puff "E" Combs? Does he know "E"?

WF: I know that his bodyguard, Wolf, knew "E".

WW: Oh, not the security. Was security not on point all the time?

WF: Wolf was not just security. He was an escort, a bodyguard. Wolf was his muscle.

WW: Does Jennifer know drow?

WF: I never witnessed her on drow.

WW: How has this affected your business?

WF: If you put my name on the search engines, see what comes up. As a result, I have been unable to find truly gainful employment. No one wants to deal with me because of this whole Puffy scandal. People depend on a driver like me to have discretion and be low key and secure. But once they do a background check and all of that stuff comes up, I don't usually get a call back. I may get the first interview, but I don't get the second.

WW: When was the last time you talked to Puffy?

WF: The last time I talked to him was when I went to his house and told him that I was not taking the rap for his gun. I had my partner waiting outside for me.

WW: How long after the incident did you go to his house?

WF: About four days after we were arrested.

WW: How long were you in jail?

WF: Seventeen hours.

WW: How long was he in jail?

WF: Seventeen hours. We were all in the same amount of time.

WW: Jen too?

WF: Jen had her Monopoly "Get Out of Jail Free" card. She was gone. But we did get the VIP treatment. They went out and got McDonald's for us.

WW: What was the mood like?

WF: Nervous. Very nervous. Puffy was pacing. In fact, it was the only time that I knew he knew my name. Until that day, he had never called my name. He would call me "Playboy," or "Yo, dog." But in the prison—he was on the outside of the holding cell, chained to a bench, and Wolf and I were on the inside—he leaned over up against the bars and said, "Yo, Woody, don't talk to nobody. Wait until you talk to the lawyers. Don't say nothing." He needed me.

WW: What was Wolf's demeanor?

WF: Wolf's demeanor was very friendly toward me too. They thought I would be down with their plan.

WW: But you saw through it right away. So somewhere along that eleven-traffic-light ride, you knew you weren't going to compromise your foundation beliefs.

WF: I didn't know I would even have to be tested. I went from being in shock to being in double shock. I had never been arrested in my life.

WW: So when you went to Puffy's house and told him you weren't going to take the rap for the gun, did you ring the doorbell? And who answered the door?

WF: He knew I was coming. And he said, "Don't worry, Wolf won't be there." Wolf and I had had some run-ins and he had threatened me a few times before this incident. And I guess Puffy thought I was coming there for the payoff.

WW: So did you ring the doorbell at his house?

WF: The doorman let me in.

WW: This is the place on Park Avenue that was on the market for sixteen million dollars? My friend Susie John, who is a listener and a friend in my head, is also a real estate person and she says it's a very, very small place—even though it's like four stories high. So you go there, does he invite you in?

WF: Uh, yeah.

WW: Does he offer you a seat?

WF: I didn't sit down. I was in there no more than three minutes.

WW: But he was offering hospitality? He wanted to lure you.

WF: He did promise to make my family comfortable. And I knew at that point that he was a snake and I had to deal with this on my own.

WW: So did he come to you with a better offer?

WF: Nope. I didn't even let the conversation go there. I came for one purpose. I said, "I cannot work for you anymore.

And I'm not going to take your gun. My daughter was totally hysterical over this situation." And he said, "Yeah, dog. I can understand all of that. But you can't be telling people that I offered you this money." And I said, "Okay."

WW: So you essentially quit your job. And your ride-out speech is "Don't tell anyone I offered you this money"? Then you turn around and you left. Did you say anything to him, like "You're pathetic!"?

WF: No, no. I just left and I had my partner waiting outside. I told my partner, "Listen, if I'm not out of there in five minutes, call nine one one. Tell them I'm being kidnapped."

WW: Wow!

WF: I had only planned to be in there no longer than five minutes.

WW: So when Shyne gets out of jail will signing with Bad Boy again be smart?

WF: I don't know. I didn't really have much to do with Shyne and that whole thing. But if you notice, during the trial the whole thing shifted toward Shyne. Now, I don't know if they had some sort of deal for it to go that way or what. But Puffy distanced himself from Shyne during the trial and basically left him out there to dry. Whether that was smoke and mirrors we will not know.

WW: I guess you're right. Thank you, Wardell!

WF: My pleasure.

WW: It was nice meeting you.

WF: Same here.

CHAPTER

8

BMs (Baby's Mamas)

omen have been trapping men since the dawn of time. But never in our history has it become so prevalent. It is more than just a strategy. Trapping men with babies and becoming baby's mamas (BMs) has become for some women a full-time profession. In the world of celebrity, the BM game is damn near an art form.

But for every success story—for every woman who has trapped a rapper, singer, athlete, or actor by having his baby, for every woman who has found wealth and a lifetime of security doing it—there is a story of pure hell. I get frequent calls from women for whom the baby-mama game has backfired and gone terribly wrong. There are stories of family court and paternity tests and worse—finding out that your superstar is really just another broke-ass nigga leaving you stuck with a baby *and* all of the bills. This happens more often than not.

A lot of girls who fall for these artists and entertainers have no idea what they are getting themselves into. They have no idea what this game is all about—and believe me, it is very much a game, particularly for many of the men. For them it's all about the conquests and racking up as many notches in their belt as they can. For many of these men, it is a game to see how many women they can play.

It is so sad to see how women allow themselves to be treated just for the hope, the possibility, of being Mrs. Celebrity. And yes, for a lot of these girls it is about being the "one." It is very much in their minds that they will be the special lady whom he takes home, with whom he settles down. This, too, is fantasy. Too often, the woman is looked upon as little more than a groupie. And getting pregnant, more often than not, will not guarantee that he will marry and settle down. It just may cause so much animosity that the relationship could border on abuse—which can come in many forms.

The mother of three of the alleged eleven children of Old Dirty Bastard, who is now calling himself Dirt McGirt and may be calling himself something else by the time this book comes out, has a sad story. She used to call me on a regular basis at the radio station. One particular time, I was talking about him on the air and she called up on the request line. Do you know how hard it is to get on the request line, how many times she had to call back and then hold on? But she wanted to talk. I didn't put her on the air. I had Art, my producer, play a couple of songs while I talked to her behind the scenes.

She told me Old Dirty was driving around in a big-body Benz while owing thirty-five thousand dollars in back child support. She could barely feed her kids. And this woman was calling me just to kvetch. And I must tell you, this story is very common.

I did an interview with Craig Mack's baby's mama in the studio. She flew all the way from Chicago to do the show. And she was saying the same thing—no child support, blah, blah, blah. I was kind of shocked to hear all of this.

There are many baby's mama horror stories of men of means turning their backs on the seeds they planted and leaving children damn near destitute. And it's not only in rap. Karl Malone, NBA All-Star and one of the fifty greatest players ever, walked out on his twins and didn't acknowledge them until very recently. Their life growing up was very different from the millionaire status their father and his other children have enjoyed.

But when the BM game is played correctly, a woman can sit back and never have to worry about another dime as long as she lives. Exhibit A: Kim Porter.

Kim Porter is the Baby's Mother of the Millennium. If you are going to be a BM, she has written the blueprint. For women like Kim, who have no other niche in society, don't know how to make a dollar any other way, being a BM at the scale of a Kim Porter is the best route to take. If you're going to do it, do the damn thing! Go to the Kim Porter Baby's Mother School and take Course 101: How to Land a Rich One. And if at first you don't succeed, try, try again.

Kim Porter arrived in New York City on the back of hotshot producer Dallas Austin (who produced many of the hits of TLC, including a baby with Chili). He wasn't a big name then. He and Kim knew each other from Atlanta. Dallas was coming to the Big Apple and somehow Kim managed to be right there with him. She landed a job as a receptionist for Uptown Records, which at that time, in the early 1990s, was the hippest label in America—home to an up-and-coming Sean "Puffy" Combs and acts Jodeci and Mary J. Blige.

At this time, I was the queen of nighttime radio on 98.7 KISS, which was slaying everybody up and down the dial. And I was the KISS "it" girl. Puffy was an intern, moving into head of A & R at Uptown. From what I understand, he tried to holler at Kim

Porter back then, but who was he? He didn't have any real money, he wasn't fabulous. Al B. Sure, however, was "it." He had "Nite & Day," and was every young girl's dream. And miss honey got with that and trapped it. She zeroed in on her target and produced a son.

When Al didn't step up to the plate and basically abandoned little Quincy, she didn't miss a beat. Kim Porter found another— not only one who would take care of her first child but one who would allow her to trap him with another. That's why she's the Baby's Mother of the Millennium. Even with her game plan out there exposed for all to see, she was still very effective.

She didn't give Puffy a second look when she first came to town. Then all of a sudden, as his star started to rise and he was becoming one of the hottest producers/acts in the business, he became very cute to her. All of a sudden he's now good enough for her. And how she did it? Scandalous. According to Misa, Puffy's first baby's mother, Kim and Misa were good friends. So while Misa's crying on Kim's shoulders, Kim is angling her way right into Puffy's life—and bed. (See exclusive interview with Misa.) But all's fair in love and hootchieness.

I used to be very judgmental toward women like Kim Porter, until I grew up and matured. I realize now that everybody cannot have a viable trade. This is America, where anything is possible for anybody. Formal education is not for everybody. Everybody cannot be a plumber, a welder, or a hairdresser. Some people have a gift of a sexy walk and being pretty. And they're so lazy and shifty in their movements that they decide, "Why expand my mind when I can be with a man and have him take care of me?" And if you're going to take that route, ride it well. And Kim Porter does it well. She has turned being a baby's mom into a full-time profession. She figured it out. Good for her.

And I'm going to tell you a secret: Men are weak. They are weak to the flesh. I don't care whether it's a brilliant Einstein or a dumb schmuck, there is one thing that weakens men and that is the flesh. As strong as they pretend to be, they can always be broken down. I know it. And the Kim Porters of the world definitely know it. And, ladies, if you didn't know it, you know it now.

But if you're not careful, this Baby's Mama game can definitely backfire. If you don't trap the right man, you could be left with a bundle and *you* can end up being trapped. It's one of the chances you take.

And for those who do judge these women and look down your noses at them, fall back. There would not be a BM game to run if men weren't so damned unscrupulous. If they weren't out there running around like tomcats, if they were faithful and took even the slightest precautions when dealing with women, there wouldn't be any baby's mamas. If a man finds himself trapped, having a baby he didn't plan on with a woman he barely knows, it is his own damned fault.

Men are so sloppy with theirs that it's a wonder that there aren't more scandals. Hell, Kobe Bryant could have been dealing with a baby along with the rape charges. He didn't use a condom. Men seem so anxious that they don't step back for one minute to use that head between their ears.

If I were a man, I would never use a condom that some girl pulled out of her purse. I don't care how well I knew her. Poking pins in a condom is the oldest trick in the book. And screwing so hard that the condom falls off is another old trick. And don't fall for "I'm on the pill." Shiiiit. Another old trick. If I were a man, not only would I have my own condom but I would pull out before I was ready to cum—just to make sure. I would use intercourse just for the "in and out" experience, but I would splash off on her back or in her mouth or in her hair. You might be laughing when you read this, but I say it with a very serious face.

Let's be real. A man who has a child with a woman—even a woman who trapped him—has a responsibility to pay. I repeat, it's *his* responsibility.

Kim Porter's first baby's daddy, Al B. Sure, didn't pay. His career died. Al was successful in his twenties. Usually men don't snap into place until they are in their thirties. That's when they become more responsible. She's lucky that she found somebody like Puffy. I'm not saying Puffy is the greatest, but I have never heard anyone say he wasn't a good father to his children. Even with Misa and arguing about the money, his being a bad father was not an issue. He pays his child support. Five thousand dollars a month—which is what it was estimated Misa was getting before taking him to court—is good money. But not when you're sending your son to a twenty-five-thousand-dollar-a-year school and security detail costs about another hundred thousand because dear old dad decided to put him in all of his clothing ads and have him in on his MTV specials and everybody knows what he looks like.

Puffy accepts Kim's Quincy—her son with Al B. Sure. Then he goes on to have a child with her, Christian. He hasn't married her. Being faithful? Hmm. I don't know what I can really say about that. I just remember J.Lo coming into play somewhere during that relationship.

But the question, people, is why should he marry her? She's very accepting, apparently, of everything and everybody around him. She's the doormat, in my opinion. This is the problem with the Baby's Mother of the Millennium title. As you get older and the chippies get younger, you run out of options. You have based your livelihood on what you can do with and for your man. But is he really your man?

Kim Porter says she is a model. But have you seen her in anything? She's not a model, she's a professional shopper, and she sure knows how to run those pockets, honey. And I don't blame her. Run those pockets, Kim!

She did well for herself. And as her looks fade and she gets older she may not always have Puffy—he might turn to someone younger or more beautiful. But she has his baby. And even bigger than that, she has a son. Only women who have given birth to a son would understand what I'm saying. She has his *son*. And she will always be taken care of.

Misa has Puffy's first son. But Misa's mistake—and I actually wouldn't call it a mistake—but she failed Baby's Mother School Course 101, because she moved on and made a life for herself. And she got married—that's the quickest way to lose out in the BM game.

I have heard many guys say that marriage changes the whole game. Guys who were so good about child support in the beginning, all of sudden as soon as that baby's mama starts dating, starts getting serious with another man and eventually gets married, he starts acting funny with the money. He doesn't want that other guy lapping off any of the extra money he is giving that baby's mama.

It's not right. But I understand. And it seems to be that way with Puffy and Misa. You cannot give me a good reason why he hasn't made her child support in line with what he is giving Kim Porter or why he hasn't made it in line with inflation, even. Or in line with his earning abilities, which have increased dramatically since Justin was born.

Should Misa have remained single and dependent? I mean, look, she was getting somewhere in the neighborhood of five thousand dollars a month. And Kim Porter is reportedly getting about five to eight times that amount every single month. (Kim Porter took Puffy to court a couple of a years ago to prove paternity, and under their settlement agreement the exact amount she is receiving was undisclosed.)

Kim Porter is playing the baby's mama game very well. "Give up the money, or I'm blowing the whistle." Blowing the whistle on what? I don't know. But I do know that she can't be Puffy's woman without knowing some secrets. And that's Course 102 in the BM School: Use every advantage to stay ahead of the game.

Personally, I believe that a baby's mama should move on and work on building a life for herself and her child apart from the dad, à la Misa Hylton-Brim. In some circles, a woman who can do this actually gains the respect of the father.

I spoke with Suge Knight about the issue. He has four children by four different women—very sloppy, in my opinion. But he's managing it all. Unlike some men, Suge would prefer the mother of his children to move on. He is even willing to pay for the wedding!

SK: *You know, to me, it's like a lot of women that I done messed with and dated had a baby. But the most important thing is for them to get married. And I used to tell them all the time, "Get married. I'll pay for the wedding."*

WW: (Laughs.) *Just leave me the hell alone!*

SK: *I'll walk you down the aisle; I'll give you the biggest gift.*

Because it's nothing worse than having an ex who's not involved with anybody.

WW: *Meanwhile, you go on and get married and then they're miserable and they're calling—*

SK: *Or you know, you're just trying to do your thing. Either you're working or you wanna date or whatever you wanna do, and they're like stalking you. You at the movies and they stalking you. You go in here and they stalking you. But if you don't get them to get somebody and they don't have somebody . . . you know they always gonna be the ones that mess with you.*

WW: *Yes.*

SK: *But if they got somebody, they gotta calm it down because they don't want they hubby or—*

WW: *Yes, yes—*

SK: *—they dude to see what's going on. So the best thing for any ex is to have somebody to keep 'em away from you.*

To get involved or not to get involved is one of those rules that depends very much on the man. But here are some other rules to consider if you plan on being a baby's mama:

RULE NO. 1:
Get the celebrity name on the birth certificate.

This seems like a no-brainer. But a lot of women get pregnant by rappers or entertainers or athletes who may already be married, and getting the man's name on the birth certificate may not be so simple. Nevertheless, it will save you a lot of time on the back end if you do this first. Still, there are no guarantees.

RULE NO. 2:
Don't expect acknowledgment.

Just because you named the kid Celebrity Jr., don't expect the man to claim him. Case in point: Actor and former rapper Ice-T had a one-night stand with a girl in the Bronx. She got pregnant and named the baby Tracy Morrow Jr., thinking that would force Ice-T to pay up and step up as a father. It took years and many court battles and DNA tests for Ice-T to finally pay. He still doesn't acknowledge the child. Is the baby's mama set for life? Probably. Was it worth it? Probably.

RULE NO. 3:
Don't get pregnant by a married celebrity.

Preferably you want to get hooked up with a man who is available, someone who will at least put you in his starting-five rotation. You want to make sure you are on that list to spend time with during the holidays, birthdays, etc. You will never be on that list if the star you've trapped is married. You will never be anything except a sore topic in his mind. You will never be number one and will not live the lifestyle you may have dreamed of living.

RULE NO. 4:
Get pregnant by someone who has a future.

This also seems like a no-brainer, but the reality is that all that glitters certainly isn't gold, or platinum or diamonds. Many of these so-called stars are broke. He may have a hit record today but be one busted single away from being dropped from his label. And then what?

If you're going to hook up with a star, make sure it's someone like a 50 Cent, a Lebron James, or even an Ice Cube, someone with endorsements, a multideal contract, movie deals, and a future. Otherwise, you could end up with one huge headache and a baby.

A mature man, someone with some years in his game, is preferable to a newbie, someone fresh in the game. You want to hook up with someone with a lot to lose so that even if you aren't in his starting five, even if you aren't on his A-team, even if you violate Rule No. 3 and he is married, you will be well taken care of just to keep quiet. Michael Jordan had a little baby scare a few years ago and his wife, Juanita, was going to leave him. Remember that? Well, the Jordans worked things out and you haven't heard a peep from the woman crying pregnant, have you? I bet she is luxuriating right now.

A man with a clean reputation, or at least a very Hollywood family image, would be even better. He would do just about anything to keep the news about your little bundle a secret.

RULE 5:
Find out how many other kids he has.

And also, find out how he is taking care of his other children before you even have sex with him. The last thing you want to do is accidentally get pregnant by a man who is already a deadbeat dad. And if you're planning properly (and I always believe a woman should plan things out), make sure you know exactly the kind of man you are dealing with. Kim Porter didn't do her due diligence with Al B. Sure, but you better bet that she watched how Puffy doted on Justin and you better believe that it was a deciding factor before she became a BM again.

RULE 6:
Get on your grind!

Okay, you got the child support from Celebrity X. Now you have to make that money work for you. Don't just sit on your behind and luxuriate, get out and make sure you are set. Learn a craft, build a business, try to stabilize a future for yourself.

Misa Hylton-Brim is the best example of a baby's mother who got on her grind, made that money work for her, and created her own career. And look at Misa today. She's a leading stylist in her own right. She is China Doll. And you have to applaud this woman. She did not have to go out and start her own business and do her own thing. Hell, when she hooked up with Puffy she was a teenager. She was "young and dumb." And as a young person she could have easily been dazzled by all the flash that was Puffy and just totally relied on him. But she didn't. She got on her grind.

And while Misa is suing Puffy for more child support, it's not because she needs the money. As she pointed out, she can afford to pay *him* what he's paying her. But she's suing him to get what she's entitled to, and that's only fair.

RULE 7:
Keep your lifestyle clean.

Another no-brainer. But, ladies, if you aren't on the up and up it can cost you dearly. I'm not sure what the deal is with the baby's mama of Roc-A-Fella Records executive Damon Dash, but a court awarded custody of their son to Dame Dash. *He* got custody!

How tragic is that? And what does this say about the kind of mother she is that a judge would rule that he would make a better parent?

I know some of you are saying, why can't he make a good parent? Let's look at it from a very fundamental level. Even if he weren't Damon Dash and was just an ordinary man, a plumber, a teacher, a banker, he still wouldn't be a better parent than the child's mother, in my opinion. That is, unless the mother is a total mess.

By and large single men do not make good parents. And if you're a single man, taking care of children and getting the job done, I am not talking about you. But look at Dame Dash and factor in the parties, the trips, the champagne, the hos. Factor in the international playa status and you begin to get a picture of what kind of mother we're dealing with that he is more desirable.

The very basic question I have is: What must she have done to make the courts give that child to him?

I don't know, but, ladies, keep your lifestyle clean—especially if you're a baby's mama. You never want to lose custody. As long as you have custody, you have a little hold on his pockets. Lose the custody and you did all that hootchie-ing and plotting for nothing.

RULE NO. 8:
Get the goodies in your name!

This may be the most important. You will learn that things can turn for you at a moment's notice, and you never know when he wants to get nasty.

If the house, the cars, and everything are in his name, you basically have nothing but a baby. Make sure everything is in your name. Also, make sure you stash a little (or even more) from each child support check—just in case. Even a baby's mama needs some fuck-you money. Actually, a baby's mama needs that more than anyone else. You definitely need to make sure you have some money for a rainy day, because when you're a baby's mama, the rain falls fast and furious.

9

Misa Hylton-Brim, the Mother of Justin

Misa and I met on a very chilly fall night in 2003 at a public spot in Manhattan. She came by herself and pulled up in a white Navigator. She was on time. Misa was charming in her burgundy-and-light-blue Von Dutch baseball hat, pulled down low. Her hair was drawn back, colored in a beautiful shade of deep red. She had on a burgundy Juicy velour couture sweatsuit. And she was dripping in diamonds. Not for nothing, we looked like two fabulous women having a great time.

We drank martinis and before she would allow me to turn on the tape recorder for the interview, she wanted to have a conversation with me. The conversation basically went like this: "Wendy, what are you going to ask me? Wendy, what are you going to ask me? Wendy, what are you going to ask me?"

By the time she finished with her interview of me, I was exasperated. I wanted to dunk her head in water and say, "You know what, forget it! Damn you!" But I endured. She finally conceded and allowed me to turn on the recorder. And the next chapter is what we talked about.

I first met Misa Hylton-Brim when she was just Misa, a high-school girl who was Puffy's girl. I didn't know she was in high school. She was mature and sophisticated even back then. Puffy was the intern at Uptown Records who moved quickly up the ranks to become head of A & R. He was responsible for pushing Jodeci and Mary J. Blige to success and as their stars rose, so did his. Puffy seemed to be everywhere back then (and not much has changed). And wherever you saw Puffy, there was Misa by his side. You may remember her as the young lady with the short blond hair in Biggie's video "Big Poppa." She's in the Jacuzzi next to Puffy.

As Puffy became more famous in his own right and became grist for my mill, I became persona non grata—someone to be avoided. But Misa never avoided me. While other folks were heading in the other direction when they would see me coming at events or parties, Misa always had a warm smile and a sincere hello for me.

She eventually grew into more than Puffy's armpiece. She became a stylist. She styled many of Puffy's early groups, like Jodeci and Mary. And on occasion I would talk about some of the outfits she styled or would mention her in some fashion sense on my show. In addition to gossip, fashion is always a topic of discussion on my show, and it was that way back in the day as well.

Then Misa gave birth to Puffy's son and all of a sudden she became more of a fixture in hip-hop culture. She not only had a baby with a man who was fast becoming one of the most power-ful men in hip-hop, but she began also to step up her styling ca-reer. She started styling Lil' Kim, and Lil' Kim was becoming just as famous for her outlandish outfits, like the mink bikini, as she was for her rap.

I would see Misa at the VH1 Fashion Awards and we would finger-wave, which to me is the friendliest kind of wave you could give. And no matter where I would see Misa, she was always cordial. Even when she was with Puffy—who to this day might shade me out—Misa has always managed to be civil, if not more than civil, with a two-cheek kiss, then a nice smile from across the room.

She's been civil even when I haven't been. For example, there was a story that came to me about Misa in a club with Baby from Cash Money. The rumor had it that Baby was in town attending a birthday party that was being thrown for him. He was being his very Negroidian self with the Cristal bottles lined up and a stack of hundred-dollar bills on the table. Allegedly Misa was throwing herself all over him, which is scandalous only because she's a married woman. I talked about it on the radio. I had to. It is an incident that Misa completely denies. (See following exclusive interview.)

There were also rumors about Misa being involved in some sort of triangle with Missy Elliott and rapper Trina (something which she addresses and denies in our exclusive interview). I was hyping it up on the show, getting ready to talk about it in the four o'clock hour, when all of a sudden there was a special delivery to the station. I open it and there is a fabulous pink Fendi scarf (she knows I love pink) and the most motherly tear-jerking note basically saying, "Look, I'm on the PTA. I am a carpool mom. . . ." She's pulling out all of the mother stuff. And it got me. I had to tell my audience, "Guys, I'm not going to tell this story." She weakened me with the kryptonite: "Wendy, mother to mother . . . Wendy, I'm a mom."

And I never repeated the rumor and I won't do it here either. She got me again with "Wendy, mother to mother . . ." when I read from the *Daily News* a story about her son, Justin. It was a story about his new school—a very private school in Manhattan. It was twenty-five thousand dollars a year. He needed a security detail—it was all straight from the newspaper. And I read it on the air. I talked about how all of the other kids at the school were rich but he's rich *and* famous *and* the son of Puffy. I got a call from Misa during the show saying, "Wendy, mother to mother . . ." That gets me all the time. And she knows this. I don't know how she knows this. Maybe it is a mother thing. She said, "Mother to mother, please don't say anything more about Justin and where he goes to school."

I said, "Misa, but it's in the newspaper." She didn't realize that.

"Well, Puffy is freaking," she said.

I could tell Puffy isn't pleased at all that Misa and I are friendly. If he could, he would definitely have put a stop to that a long time ago. There are people who want to be friendly with me in his camp but can't. Misa, to her credit, has never buckled to that pressure. She has always been her own woman. And even in her soft-spoken, gentle manner, you get a sense that she does exactly what she wants to do.

I got to know her better recently while working on *The Cook-out*, a film produced by Queen Latifah. Misa was hired as the stylist for the film, which is scheduled for release in the summer of 2004. The movie was directed by Lance "Un" Rivera, who was Biggie's manager and Lil' Kim's manager at one point. (In December of 1999 "Un" was stabbed at the Kit Kat Klub in New York by Jay-Z at an album release party for Q-Tip. According to published reports, a fight broke out in the VIP section over some alleged bootlegging of a Jay-Z album, *Vol. 3: Life and Times of S. Carter*. Jay-Z avoided jail time with a plea bargain and a six-hundred-thousand-dollar payoff to "Un," who apparently has moved on to bigger and better things.)

Queen Latifah offered me a small part in *The Cookout,* and Misa had to style my character. You know me and my body issues. I hate working with stylists because they think every big girl—which I am—wants to dress like Queen Latifah or the even bigger girl, Mo'Nique from *The Parkers,* or Star Jones from *The View.*

All of these women dress great for them, but I wanted a particular style. And I thought, "Oh, I can't act like Greta Garbo," having her pull twenty-five outfits for this tiny part of mine. I mean, it was a very small role playing a TV reporter. I'm not an actress. I was told I would be playing someone true to character; I would be basically playing myself.

Misa had it figured out from the start. She said, "Wendy, I see you as this sexy TV reporter and you'll be in a sexy pantsuit." And I immediately thought, "Oh, my gosh! A pantsuit! There's potential for me to look like Rosie O'Donnell!" You remember when Rosie used to do her talk show and she used to come out with those lesbianic suits and those *How You Doin'?* shoes?

Misa ended up pulling this fabulous pinstripe suit for me. I put it on and it fit perfectly and I wanted to kiss her, throw her up in the air, catch her, and kiss her again. I felt so comfortable on the set and at the end of it I asked, "Misa, the tags are still on the suit, can I buy it from you?" She said, "Wendy, you can have it." Isn't that great?

We kept in touch after that. Misa's the keep-in-touch type of person who will call you just to see how you're doing. When it came time to do this book, I thought she would make a great subject to be interviewed. I wanted to have exclusive talks with people folks have not heard from but whose story they might be interested in knowing. And Misa Hylton-Brim is a woman with a story.

I called her and, thank God, like me, she is a person who never changes her cell phone number. (In the hip-hop world, it's not at all unusual for an artist to change his or her number every month.)

"Can we talk?" I said. "We can make it private; we can make it secret. I will not tell Puffy. He will not know about this interview until the book is out." (Because that nigga probably would have stopped it.)

The pièce de résistance, and the reason why she was so eager to tell her story, is that about two days before I called her it was printed in the New York *Daily News* that she was taking Puffy to court for more child support. She had not gotten an increase in her child support since she'd had Justin ten years before. In the meantime, Kim Porter—Baby's Mother of the Millennium—was just luxuriating.

Since our interview, a Manhattan court judge has ordered Puffy to cough up financial data to Misa's legal team. That info had been deep undercover since he settled a paternity suit with Kim Porter in 2001, when he was granted joint custody and would have to pay up until Christian turned twenty-one. The judge also denied Puffy's request to be referred to only by his initials in court documents to avoid unwanted publicity over the paternity suit. So we will be staying tuned to all of the details in this case.

And, no, Misa doesn't want Puffy back—she's happily married with two more children—but what's fair is fair. When you read what she has to say, you're going to understand.

She doesn't tell all in this interview and she doesn't put Puffy on blast. She is guarded and at some points it's like pulling teeth getting her to talk, which I understand. While we are friendly and while I am a woman of my word, maybe Misa didn't know how far she could confide in me. I promised not to disclose that she was doing this interview for my book. But I know somewhere inside, just in case, she felt she needed to hold back. So we met and she talked cautiously.

She didn't talk badly about Puffy. But she did talk honestly. Misa does have a story to tell and she does plan on writing a tell-all book, and has asked if I would interview her for it. So that's coming. I got from her what I could—which in my opinion was juicy enough to make me wonder what else she really has. I can't wait to find out.

EXCLUSIVE INTERVIEW SESSION
Misa Hylton-Brim

MHB: You're too eager

WW: I am.

MHB: I have stepdaughters fifteen and ten. They had heard you talking about me on the radio and they were upset. They asked their father, "Daddy, why is this being said?"

WW: You're talking about the story about you and Baby [from Cash Money Millionaires].

MHB: Baby invited me to his birthday party. When I got there, we talked a little business. He told me, "My kids' birthdays are coming up and I want to get a pink mink bedspread for my daughter and a blue one for my son. Can you make that happen?" So that's what we were talking about. Then you said I was on his lap at the club. And that's not how I carry myself.

WW: That was me. It was very chicken-headish and I'll tell you what—

MHB: And you said you felt sorry for me . . . and I was saying to myself, "I got a job. I am creating something for this guy's kids, and it gets turned all around that I'm having this affair and am acting out with him in a club—which did not happen. And then I have to explain it to my stepchildren . . . that was tough.

WW: When you create something like that for an artist, do they pay you or do you get guarantees for the next video?

MHB: I don't do that.

WW: I hate the double standards. And it's not going to go away. Women, I guess, we're suspect unless we do anything other than staying away from men.

138

MHB: That situation showed me I can't talk to anybody.

WW: You must have been wearing something skimpy.

MHB: You want to know what I had on? I had just come from Miami and I had on an Iceberg sweater, it was mint green. And I had on white Iceberg jeans, those white leather-looking jeans. I had on a pair of sneakers and a white leather jacket.

WW: So you were covered up.

MHB: My hair looked like I just came from the pool. I literally just got off the plane. I pulled it up and stuck a pin in it.

WW: You're naturally pretty. So it looks like you're always done up.

MHB: Thank you. There were pictures. I wasn't . . . and believe it or not, I don't dress skimpy. If you really watch how I dress, I don't.

WW: Your subjects do.

MHB: [Lil'] Kim's the only one.

WW: You've done Foxy too.

MHB: Oh, yeah. Foxy will dress skimpy. But Kim was like the extreme. The most extreme.

WW: What ever happened to your boutique?

MHB: Madison Star? That's my daughter's name and the name of my brand, and things kept falling through. Different business partners kept dropping out. And me trying to do this on my own has been extremely hard. I don't have any support from anyone who can really support me and put me out there. So it's been hard. I've been doing everything on my own. A lot of people looking from the outside would assume Puffy would be there helping me or should be there helping me. A lot of people really haggle me with my money and fees because they think, "She doesn't really need it."

WW: I would assume that Puffy is helping you. And not helping you from the perspective of banging you. Because I don't believe that you guys have that kind of relationship at all. But I believe he is helping you to benefit his number-one son, Justin. Not number one because he favors Justin. But number one because that's his first son, the restaurant chain, the diamond, the oldest. Puffy could write you a check every month and you would never have to work again. Would you be okay with that?

MHB: I think the type of person I am, I would always have to do something. I don't know how to be a rich man's wife. And I don't know how to not do anything but sit in the house. I don't know how to do that.

WW: Well, how did you grow up, not knowing how to do these things? I'm curious.

MHB: I would say middle class. My mom and dad split up when I was about six or seven. I grew up around a lot of women, a lot of working women, taking care and handling business.

WW: Your mom is Asian and your father is black?

MHB: My mother is Japanese and black.

WW: Does your mother look more Asian than black? So you had a lot of Asian traditions in your house?

MHB: Yes. That's funny, I was talking to a friend of mine who is mixed. Asian women by nature have a lot of tradition, a very Joy Luck Club thing. But of course, I would be the different one, not to be raised in the traditional route. But obviously my grandma wasn't traditional, either, because she married a black man. So I was talking to a friend of mine who said, "I can't do anything right!" Because her family is very strict.

WW: When you were in high school, you met Puffy?

MHB: No. I knew Puffy since I was a little girl. He lived around the corner from my best friend. We used to hang around in the same neighborhood, but didn't physically play with each other.

WW: I saw "Driven: Notorious B.I.G." He was fabulous. A bit on the flashy side back then. Very cute, by the way. Just to document how fabulous he was back then.

MHB: He is five years older than me, so back then he was thirteen and I was eight. His sister I knew a little more—Keisha.

WW: She used to be a secretary at Bad Boy or something. Why isn't she talked about more?

MHB: She's quiet and to herself. She doesn't have to be seen, I guess. She's very quiet.

WW: So how did you finally meet Sean, the older man?

MHB: How did we date? I met him at a Kwame concert. It was my very best friend's birthday and we were out to see Kwame for her birthday. And we were all talking and [Puffy] was asking for my number. I couldn't stand him. He was so arrogant. That's so weird. His mouth. Oh, my God, you would just look at the phone and say, "I don't believe this!"

WW: He was the intern then at Uptown. Cocky. Commuting back and forth from Howard. Did you ever go to the campus?

MHB: Yeah. And it took about a year. I told him I was older than what I was. I always lied about my age. I always wanted to be older. Now I'm grown, I say, "I wish I could be younger."

WW: The thing about being grown is if you can't bring a thirtysomething head with a twenty-something age, then it's not worth it. I wouldn't turn back the hands of time.

MHB: Me either.

WW: And I'm looking forward to what life has in store. Every day I feel I'm getting stronger as a woman—professionally and personally.

MHB: Mm-hmm.

WW: So where'd you guys go on your first date?

MHB: Our first date? I don't remember the first date.

WW: Puffy, he took you to your senior prom?

MHB: He surprised me in a suit and Andre Harrell's convertible Mercedes.

WW: How much were bitches hating on you?!!!!!!

MHB: (*Laughter.*) I didn't know they were. It sounds so crazy. But it didn't seem to me like that at the time. That was my life. It was normal. It was nice. He surprised me. It's not like I had never been in a Benz before.

WW: Were you at City College? He and Heavy D came to my radio show to promote that. I was supposed to be one of the hype girls—I would say cheerleader, but I've never been cool enough to be a cheerleader. So I was supposed to be one of the girls on the sidelines for that game. But when I got there it was chaos, I mean chaos, outside, and I had no idea what was going on inside. You were with him at that time at City College.

MHB: Yes.

WW: Jessica Rosenbloom was the woman who was the promoter with Puffy on that. She's also gone on to promote a lot of big events here in New York City. Cordial words for her now?

MHB: Jessica and I are very cordial. She used to rub me the wrong way. You know how some people have that kind of energy. I used to try to go into The Tunnel with my twenty girlfriends. And she would always give me a problem. But that was ten years ago.

WW: Jessica left him to be the fall guy for a lot of shit, didn't she, in your opinion?

MHB: Um.

WW: He was an easy mark. Black, male, dumb, New York City. Hip-hop.

MHB: That's when we lived in Hackensack.

WW: Geez! At that point, he really had no cachet.

MHB: He wasn't broke. He was probably six figures, maybe just under. At least ninety thousand dollars. He had the A & R position. VP. Now you understand what I mean about everything.

       We used to hang out a lot with Russell [Simmons] and Andre [Harrell] on the weekends. That's when they would have these big parties in the Cloisters and I would go there for the weekend.

WW: So back when they were having parties in the Cloisters in New Jersey and you were going to the house and seeing people like Naomi Campbell and Russell and Andre were there and these were their houses, would you feel intimidated? Would Puffy treat you equally or would he leave you in a corner?

MHB: He would treat me equally.

WW: Did you make friends with some of the girls?

MHB: Yes.

WW: That's on your own.

MHB: He would introduce me to some people—and whether he had dated them or not, he better not bring them around me because I wasn't having it.

WW: You knew what this business was about when you signed on.

MHB: I didn't know. But I learned.

WW: Some of the women he would bring you around—

MHB: I'm not going into that now. I'm saving that for later.

WW: Wow! Misa . . . I hear you. But it takes a certain type of woman to see the writing on the wall and know what the game is.

MHB: I'll never forget, one time we had a party—and we had a lot of parties in our home—

WW: —in the home you shared with Puff?

MHB: Yes.

WW: Where was that home?

MHB: Scarsdale [New York].

WW: Fabulous.

MHB: Down the street from where I live now.

WW: So you're still doing very well

MHB: I try. I've had some ups and downs.

WW: So you'd have parties at your home that you shared with Puffy in Scarsdale?

MHB: And I remember one party, girls were walking around, women everywhere, they all wanted him. And I couldn't do it. But that was my life. It was normal. It wasn't that serious. Maybe I was young. Maybe I couldn't do it now. Maybe I was naïve.

WW: Were you looking at other men, while he was doing—

MHB: No.

WW: I don't understand, either, how you put up with it. Did you date popular guys, the high school football captain? Or was this your introduction to popularity?

MHB: I dated mostly street guys, thugs. You know what's funny? A lot of things that happened to me in my life just happened. I would get boyfriends who wanted to front, or buy me this pocketbook and buy me things. But I never asked for anything. I never asked for this lifestyle. I didn't ask for anything, it just came into my lap. I had the local thug. And I don't want to say the local drug dealer because that sounds so stereotypical. But I dated guys like that. I dated a guy who had a Benz and Puffy didn't have a car and I ended up liking Puffy more. I was young and I wanted to date him.

WW: You were in the popular clique in school.

MHB: Yeah, me and my friends were popular.

WW: And you dressed well—

MHB: —Yeah, the hair, big hair fetish. I would dye my hair and cut my hair on the regular.

WW: So when you and Puffy got together and you got your house in Scarsdale, that was a good life? He was what, up-and-coming with Bad Boy at the time you purchased the home?

MHB: The deal happened right before that.

WW: Where were you before, an apartment?

MHB: In Hackensack, New Jersey. A little town house/condo. He rented it.

WW: That was when Bad Boy was brand-new.

MHB: Bad Boy started in the basement of the house in Scarsdale.

WW: Did you plan Justin?

MHB: I was really scared when I found out I was pregnant.

WW: Scared of what? To tell your mother and father?

MHB: I was scared to tell everybody. I knew this was serious. And I knew that there was going to be a lot of opinions. I knew if I told him . . . I didn't know what to think. And I don't want to talk about my views on abortion, because that's not important. But I knew once I told him that it would be for real. No turning back.

WW: What was his reaction?

MHB: He was nervous; he was scared. He was happy. It was the best—my first five months.

WW: What does that mean?

MHB: He was attentive. He only went out a couple of nights a week. He said, "I'll be here with you," and he was. He lost his job at Uptown.

WW: What did Janice [Combs] say? Mom? There's a big smile on your face as you look around the room. Your body language is becoming very closed. Should I assume that this means no comment?

MHB: (*Laughter.*) Yeah.

WW: Okay, fair enough.

MHB: (*Laughter.*)

WW: So you're pregnant and Janice finds out.

MHB: Actually, we didn't tell anyone until I was like sixteen weeks [pregnant]. I was really itty-bitty then. I never forget I went to a Greek picnic. . . . We used to travel a lot. I had a lot of fun going to Atlanta and to L.A. and going to Philly and going to the Howard homecomings. We really had a good time.

WW: But you could also watch the chicken heads.

MHB: It was always like that. And I can remember all of my girlfriends—I got a hotel room for all of us and we would all crash in there. And I was like, I'm ready now. And I lifted my shirt and showed them and they said, "How were you hiding that?!" It was just a little bundle.

WW: Wow!

MHB: And then I told my mom shortly after that. But I think the key was to be far enough along that . . . it is what it is, Mom and Dad.

WW: Did she flip?

MHB: No. She was like "Oh, my God." And I understand. I have had younger cousins who have had babies and I have asked them, "Are you really ready?" Not to put them down but because you know because you've been through it. That's the way it was with my mom. Motherhood is a lot. It is a never-ending experience.

WW: So, did you ever think you and Puffy would get married?

MHB: Once again, due to my age, that's not anything that I viewed as important. It was important to my mom.

WW: Is marriage important now that you are married to JoJo [Brim] and have children by JoJo?

MHB: Two.

WW: Two children by JoJo and then Justin?

MHB: Yes.

WW: What would you say to a twenty-year-old girl who gets pregnant? Is marriage part of the picture?

MHB: It is. It's so important

WW: See, I'm married. And I try, Misa, not to sell women a bag of shit.

MHB: It's a lot of hard work.

WW: It's hard. But you don't marry some guy just because you're pregnant. That spells disaster.

MHB: Yeah, you don't do that. The key is to be responsible. This is like a fantasy comment: But try to make the right decision. Sit down and talk about planning.

WW: Had you had any thoughts—prior to Kim Porter and JoJo—that you and Puffy would get married?

MHB: In the early years? When Justin was born? (*Shakes her head no.*)

WW: No?! What about him made you not want to marry him, because face it, when we women—and I don't care how powerful we are—at the end of the day, like I always say, we are soft and pink. There are certain basic things that we might want to explore, might fantasize about. There must have been something very, very big that made you say, "No, not him."

MHB: Hmm.

WW: Is Puffy selfish?

MHB: Those things I won't comment on . . . not yet.

WW: Cruel?

MHB: No comment.

WW: Did things change after you had the baby and you were locked down, so to speak?

MHB: Well, one great thing about him is that if we went shopping

147

he would say, "What do you need, hair, nails? We're going out, we're going to have a good time." We would travel. I was like the only young black girl at nineteen with a live-in nanny.

WW: Isn't that fabulous?!

MHB: Now, looking back, yeah. But back then that was my life. That was always the plan.

WW: The nanny. Was she the fourth lady in the pew at church or did you go to an agency and she didn't know you from Adam?

MHB: The first nanny was a woman recommended to me by my aunt.

WW: Minded her own business?

MHB: Definitely. But shortly, my nanny experiences are a whole other thing. I can write a book on that subject alone. The first one missed her country and she was an older woman and wanted to go back. That was one down . . . eight more to go. It's hard.

Puffy wasn't like other men. He didn't say to me, "Why do you have that on?" He definitely liked style. And he liked to see me wear whatever made me look good. He liked to go out.

WW: So he loved you looking good, got you a nanny? This is an incredible life—Scarsdale, the nanny. Did you smoke weed back then?

MHB: I'm a mom now. (*Laughter.*)

WW: I got what you're saying (Wink, wink). Smoking weed, having fun, going to glamorous parties. At what point did you and Puffy's romantic relationship break up and become purely guardianship?

MHB: Kim Porter. That did it.

WW: What year was that?

MHB: Ninety-four.

WW: I don't like her. Let me just see your ring finger first.

MHB: This is not my wedding ring.

WW: What is that?

MHB: A rose.

WW: That's an interesting place to have a tattoo, Misa.

MHB: Puffy thought so too. Why do you think I did that? Maybe I did it that time for a reason.

WW: You got that at what point in your life?

MHB: Before I got married. He told me he would pay for me to get it removed—that I would never be married with it.

WW: What? Like no man would have you with that tattoo?

MHB: No, like that's bad luck.

WW: Just because it can never be covered? Is that your only tattoo?

MHB: You know we were the whole tattoo crew, the whole Jodeci, early nineties, Mary, and all of that.

WW: Damn. Yeah, that was back in the day. Is that your original wedding ring?

MHB: No, this is just a ring I have on.

WW: You must be real comfortable in your marriage that you can switch your rings around. I can't do that, yet. To me, it's the original ring or nothing. How long have you been married to Jo-Jo?

MHB: Six years.

WW: So. You and Puffy are together. The baby comes along. Jodeci, big. Mary, big. Bad Boy takes off. He is now the wonder boy of the industry. At what point do you start with your designing?

MHB: When I started I didn't realize that being a stylist was a job. I got to work with Jodeci on their first album.

WW: At what point do things start to take a turn for the "Oh, hell no!" with Puffy? Like, I'm not dealing with this.

MHB: We were talking about styling . . .

WW: Styling, that's right. Sorry. (*Laughter.*)

MHB: I got to work on Jodeci's first video and I used to help Puffy with that because he was a stylist too. And then I got Mary as a client and that's pretty much when my career took off.

WW: You were the baseball caps with the hair pulled through the top? You were the combat boots?

MHB: Yes. That was a spin-off of Jodeci. I can't say it was all my idea. That was some of [Puffy's] idea. And I was able to style.

WW: We were all doing it. It was great, very great. Now you're building a name for yourself. At what point did things with your relationship with Puffy turn sour? You said, Kim Porter. I didn't realize that she was in picture for such an extended period of time.

MHB: Kim was a friend of mine.

WW: What?! A friend?!

MHB: You knew.

WW: I did not know that! Look, I got a life outside you people, okay? I go home, I mind my business.

MHB: You didn't know that?

WW: I swear to goodness, I didn't know that! Let me just . . . [tell] you what I know, and you can correct me. Kim, friend of Dallas Austin in Atlanta, decides she wants to go to New York. Dallas arranges for her to be in New York, secretary at Bad Boy?

MHB: Uptown.

WW: Okay. Al B. Sure. The baby comes—

MHB: No, the baby was before she got the secretary position, that's why she got the secretary position. He was sort of a deadbeat. Yes, she was my friend. . . .

WW: He was a deadbeat back then?

MHB: He hated her so much. He was one of those stupid guys who was like "I hate her so much, I'm not going to take care of my kid." His birthday and Prince's birthday are the same day.

WW: Wow. Oh, light and curly is heartless and mean. I just wouldn't expect that from him. Listen . . . did she like poke the proverbial hole in the condom or did they have a relationship?

MHB: At that point, they had a real relationship. At that point, I had my second son and was on to my third child. When she had Christian, I was pregnant with my daughter. They called me from the room.

WW: How did you meet Kim?

MHB: One of my best friends, who is a model, who lives in St. Louis and who ended up not being such a good friend, they were friends and we would hang out and Kim would come. We would do fun things, go to parties. She would come to my home in Scarsdale.

WW: Still with Puffy?

MHB: Yes, and when I got my own place when Justin was about five months or six months in New Rochelle, she used to come to my home and say, "He's not right, he reminds me of Al. You need to take him to court."

WW: So, Kim's telling you that Puffy's no good and that he's a deadbeat. By the time you moved out of Scarsdale, did you move out because you and Puffy were broken up?

MHB: At that time Usher Raymond was working on his album and was about to come out. Something happened and we had to move. When I came from the hospital with Justin, I had to go back home with my mom and he ended up living in a hotel.

WW: Wow! Did you pop into that hotel to see what was going on?

MHB: I would go there from time to time.

WW: Did you ever catch him there with women?

MHB: We were very disconnected at this time.

WW: How old was Justin?

MHB: A month, two months. I think that disconnection from me . . . you know how something can kill your spirit. I just had to face that.

WW: Do you think Kim had designs on Puffy while trying to put a wedge between the two of you?

MHB: I don't know.

WW: Was that part of the fun with you and Kim and all of you girls and Puffy would have open relationships, you know what I'm saying?

MHB: No.

WW: That was part of the myth of you and Kim and Puffy.

MHB: Really?! Never. Not at all. [If that were the case,] we would probably all be together now. Right?

WW: I guess so.

MHB: If it was that open and we're all partying and living free. But I'm not that kind of girl.

WW: So Kim worked on creating this wedge and it ended up working.

MHB: Because I walked away. If I didn't walk away it would not have gone down like that.

WW: Did Puffy ever try to fight for you?

MHB: (*Nods her head yes.*)

WW: How extravagant did it get?

MHB: I think he fought more emotionally and mentally than materially.

WW: Like if I can't have you, I don't want anyone else to have you. That kind of testosterone fight.

MHB: Yes.

WW: So when you walked away, how soon after did you get your child support?

MHB: Three years.

WW: Three years?! Recently it was brought up that you guys have not redone child support since Justin was born ten years ago. How much had you been getting? Approximately, I heard sixty-five hundred dollars.

MHB: I don't want to talk about that, now.

WW: But you said less.

MHB: Yes, less, a lot less.

WW: So I'll say five thousand dollars and you don't acknowledge.

MHB: No.

WW: What's Janice's role once you split up?

MHB: We're very, very close now. She's like a second mother.

WW: So you're close. It took some years for that to happen.

MHB: Um. We had been close since. Don't get me wrong, we were never against each other. It was just that mother-son thing. Her first grandchild. Like "Oh, my God, this girl's the one? Are you going to get married? Are you not? She's younger than you."

       I went to college.

WW: Where did you go?

MHB: St. John's University.

WW: Did you graduate?

MHB: No.

WW: You didn't have to.

MHB: (*Laughter.*)

WW: You and Kim, how do you get along now?

MHB: We're cordial. We're civil.

WW: Why did she get so much more money than you? It's not fair on the outside looking in. I understand you work and she doesn't.

MHB: Why do you think?

WW: Because you're married to JoJo Brim and he's thinking, "No son of mine is going to get any dime extra when there's some nigga in the house who could be doing for him too!" That's what I think.

MHB: You think if we would have broken up, he would do more?

WW: That's right. Okay, you got two kids by another man. It's not like I can claim those two kids like Al B. Sure's a piece of a man. See, Al's made it easy for Puffy to come in and claim Quincy. Your kids, they have a father who is an able-bodied man who is taking care of his. If I were a man with a big ego, I understand his angle. It doesn't make it right. But I understand. When did you meet JoJo?

MHB: He's also from Mount Vernon, and I don't know when I met him exactly. He was a familiar face. I used to manage Case, remember that? And he was really close to Case.

WW: Yes! I do. Is he really cute? I have never seen him.

MHB: Yeah. A lot of people say he resembles Babyface and Pharrell. He has curly hair, strong features, really tall and thin. I thought he was a ballplayer. He's a beautiful person.

WW: He must be a strong man to put up with you being the baby's mother of such a famous man.

MHB: Oh, my God. He's such a beautiful person. You have no idea. He's on another level.

WW: How does he and Puffy get along?

MHB: Puffy has a lot of respect for him. You know how some people have a certain energy where you can't come at them crazy. It would almost be like coming at Russell crazy.

WW: Yeah. Puffy's got a lot of respect for JoJo. How do the boys get along and your daughter?

MHB: Very well. They're all like stair steps. So they're funny. I en-joy watching them. My daughter, she's such a little girl. Justin babies her. My middle son is like really hard on her and keeps on her, and then Justin and Niko are very close.

And what's funny is that they don't really fight, they don't argue. They're all treated equally.

WW: But one has a couple of restaurants.

MHB: But that's their life. They don't know anything else. You know what I mean?

WW: How crazy is that? Your kids are actually being brought up in a lifestyle that most people only dream about. Is Justin's bedroom at home all done up?

MHB: It's a normal, nice bedroom. It's not anything extra or over the top. He doesn't have a Jacuzzi in the middle of his room.

WW: How do your mother and father feel about Puffy, now?

MHB: My dad is always on my side. He's just supportive. He's a listener. He's not judgmental. My mom, I think, like his mom, ignores our problems and they stay close. If I was with Janice, she would introduce me as her daughter-in-law, Misa. My mother was at the marathon supporting Puffy. His mother was at my daughter's birthday party.

WW: Your mom's confident that your financial issues with Puffy, past, present, and future, will work out?

MHB: I think so.

WW: I have to ask you about something that I must admit you've put me in a place where I feel strange asking you, but I must ask you.

MHB: Okay.

WW: Your relationship with Missy.

MHB: (*Laughter.*)

WW: So you've heard that there was a relationship (Wink, wink). Trina somehow became a part of it. You and Missy were no longer cool. And it was Missy and Trina.

MHB: Absolutely not ! Missy is my daughter's godmother. We are really close friends. That's another thing. It's like me and Baby. It's like "What?!" When I hear these things. It's crazy.

155

So me and Missy and Trina, what was that supposed to be, a love triangle? I've known Missy since she first came out with her group. I styled her group. We go way back. We're friends and confidantes and she's actually my daughter's godmother. Mary is Justin's godmother. We went to church and everything.

WW: Are you close with Mary's husband?

MHB: I know Kendu. I wouldn't say we're close, but I know him.

WW: So what would you like in terms of Justin's future and stability, regarding Puffy? Clearly, Misa, as a married woman, your husband has a financial responsibility to your family. As a working woman, you already are doing something. But having a baby's father who also happens to be millions of dollars past being wealthy, what's his obligation to you and Justin?

MHB: No comment.

WW: When was the last time you had sex with Puffy?

MHB: A long time ago, but no comment! A very long time ago, but I don't want to talk about that. (*Laughter.*)

WW: How's Lil' Kim? When was the last time you talked to Kim?

MHB: Two Thousand.

WW: That's a long time.

MHB: Yeah. I haven't even run into her. Isn't that amazing? Almost four years.

WW: What happened with you guys?

MHB: No comment. That's business. It was great working with her, though. We had so much fun working together, especially when it was really, really good.

WW: How good was it when it was *really* good?

MHB: We had so much fun. We would travel and had a lot to do with fashion and taking risks. Magazine covers. I think that's when I got a different kind of recognition for my work.

WW: Kim also took it to another level. You had a subject that was a risk taker. All of a sudden she was becoming a draw to the Hollywood scene as well. She had grown past hip-hop or Club Cheetah on a Friday night. Kim took it someplace else and you went along for the ride. And you both supported each other.

MHB: Right.

WW: Is that repairable?

MHB: I don't have a problem with Kim.

WW: She's a Cancer, she doesn't really have a problem with you.

MHB: (*Laughter.*)

WW: Take it from me, the queen Cancer, she doesn't have a problem with you.

MHB: It seems like it.

WW: That's people whispering in her ear.

MHB: I don't have any problem with Kim.

WW: Does she owe you money?

MHB: No.

WW: I'm kind of saddened by that. Just because you guys were in a good place with each other.

MHB: Really good. You know, it's funny. I watched VH1 last night, the fabulous life of Lil' Kim. Did you see it?

WW: Nooooo!

MHB: It was cute and they showed a lot of work from when I worked with Kim. And they interviewed me for it in my office. But I was the only one who wasn't [featured] on the show.

WW: Wow.

MHB: (*Laughter.*) And I'm like, this is *all* my work. Not even recently; I wouldn't even say in the last two years. It was all like that.

WW: I'll tell you what, though, Misa—

MHB: —I was like, "That's not nice!" (*Laughter.*)

WW: Not only that . . . but I believe, and I don't hate on Kim, I just feel that as though Kim and a lot of people like Kim give people pipe dreams about what this business is made of. Kim is the brokest-wealthiest-looking person I know. That's all I'm saying. I'm not hating, I'm simply saying. Why does she always seem broke to me even though it seems like she has a whole bunch of stuff going on?

MHB: She seems broke to you?

WW: Yes. No comment from Misa. She's just rubbing her chin and nodding. Not nodding in agreement but listening and nodding. Is there anything else you want to talk about? There are a couple of more things I wanted to ask you about Puff (*How You Doin'*?!) but all of a sudden I don't feel as though they are appropriate. It's not ... see, I know how to behave myself. Has JoJo ever had an affair on you?

MHB: Never.

WW: Have you ever had an affair on him?

MHB: Never.

WW: Is marriage forever?

MHB: It is for me.

WW: Through thick and through thin. Any more children?

MHB: I love babies. I don't know, because it takes such a toll on me. I get really, really, really sick. I gain at least eighty pounds. My daughter is five. This is the first time I haven't been pregnant in a long time. This is different for me.

WW: Wow. Did you have breast implants?

MHB: (*Laughter.*)

WW: You and Mary and Kim on the package deal?

MHB: (*Laughter!*) No, I don't.

WW: Have you?

MHB: No. I want some now, though.

WW: It's not so bad, Misa. If you've got the money, then fund it. Eve, wouldn't you love to style her?

MHB: I might love the experience. But I don't think I want to style artists anymore.

WW: Okay. Why?

MHB: I've done that for thirteen years. I love the movies, I like the dining. I love working on bigger projects. Like I did the diva lines. Born to divas. I worked with those girls. When it's over, it's over. I've been working with Chris Rock and Serena [Williams]. So I want to switch up my clients a little bit. The music industry is so different now. But I think Eve is doing her thing. And she is the fashion "it" girl.

WW: Instead of styling Eve the artist, you would rather do the Eve TV show?

MHB: Yeah, yeah.

WW: What would you say, Misa . . . and we're practically done, you've been fabulous. But what would you say to that seventeen, that twenty-year-old girl at the party and she sees him, you know the one from the videos across the room. She wants to meet him. What advice would you give to girls like that?

MHB: (*Long pause.*) I would tell her to get to know him first. Look beyond the exterior. You may think he's cute and he may be a rapper or a singer—

WW: —and wealthy.

MHB: —and wealthy. But it's important to get to know anybody. And that goes for a guy who doesn't have anything. I think that we have expectations on people and that's how we get disappointed.

WW: Yes. I am really shocked about you and Puff and what I read in the New York *Daily News* about child support issues. I know you guys have, and will always, handle that. But it's sloppy, though. And that's his fault and not yours. You, from what I've been told, had been trying your very best to handle them—your child-support issues—in a very quiet way. It was so ghetto. You know what I'm sayin'? You black folks are beyond that. By the way, we call Kim Porter, on my radio show, the chicken head of the millennium.

MHB: (*Laughter.*)

WW: (*Laughter.*)

MHB: Why don't you think people like her? What is it?

WW: I think the thing about Kim Porter that people question is that "Dallas Austin—I want to go to New York to be in the big city." The Al B. Sure, Puffy. Everything is like so freaking methodical with her. And not for nothing, and you can use looks as a part of this, she always looks like she's ready to fuck somebody up. Her look. She's got a very intimidating look.

MHB: You think?

WW: I do. Come on! Puffy was sipping on J.Lo. He was with J.Lo when he was with Kim Porter. She's like his ride-or-die ghetto stallion—have the baby, stand by her man. You know what I'm sayin'? People look at that as an old-fashioned ghetto tale, except with more money at the end of it.

Misa, I think, at least I look at you as a woman who met a young boy when you were a young girl. And you went on and you made your own life. Including getting married to a man named JoJo and having other children. I look at you as being removed from that foolishness right now. Puffy's got his own thing going on. Kim Porter? She'll be around forever. She's not skilled.

MHB: (*Laughter.*)

WW: You know what I'm sayin'? She'll be around until the end of time with him. And put up, it appears to me, with whatever he's willing to dish out, because she has no other way.

I guess my question to you ultimately is: Is Kim Porter a chicken head?

MHB: I don't want to call her names or judge her.

WW: Okay.

MHB: Remember when I gave you that scarf?

WW: Yes. It was a pink scarf.

MHB: And you said, "She probably got that for free"? I didn't. I was like "She just shot my little gift down."

WW: You bought it?

MHB: Yes.

WW: I still have it.

MHB: You think I'm like everybody else.

WW: Yes. I'm sorry.

MHB: Do you still think that?

WW: No.

MHB: Why?

WW: Because you came here tonight.

MHB: You would have thought I said I was coming and then wouldn't show up?

WW: Yes.

MHB: Really?!

WW: Yes. I thought you would share tonight with a bunch of other girls in your cipher and then the haters. You know. And they would have been like "Oh, fuck her!"

MHB: You know what's funny? I know everybody would be really surprised, because I used to get really upset. And I wouldn't let your show be on in my office. It couldn't be on in my car. People who sit in my car waiting for me had to change the station before I got in. Because I didn't want to hear the things you were saying. And if I didn't hear them, I couldn't get upset. And mess up my day. So, I felt differently as time went on. And I think you've also changed.

WW: I have.

MHB: I think it's kind of therapeutic for things that used to make me so angry. And then for me to sit here with you tonight, it's okay.

WW: It's not the worst, Misa.

MHB: No, it's not the worst. And things are going to be what they're going to be. And I know sometimes I'm too nice, or too trusting. And whatever you do, that will come back to you.

WW: I didn't know that. I'm painting you with the same brush that I paint them—hard and calculating and so on and so forth. I consider myself as an outsider in this business.

MHB: I do too.

WW: You don't see me hanging with the Baby and the Cash Money Millionaires and all of them. I—first of all, there was a point where I wasn't invited to all of that. But now, I guess by virtue of cachet, I get invited to stuff all the time. But it's too late. I've already discovered life outside the industry and I love it. I just talk about you people. I'm putting you in with them now. I comment on you people and what goes on in your lives. I really don't live it. And when you say things to me like "mother to mother . . ." that works.

MHB: I was sincere.

WW: I know you were, but that's like my kryptonite. That's my kryptonite.

MHB: I'm not like them. I'm among them but not of that same thing. I've always been raised like that. Different things are important to me.

WW: Does JoJo . . . his position is with Def Jam. . . .

MHB: Now he does consulting. But he was director of A & R for R & B.

WW: So he's able to contribute to taking care of you and your boys and your little girl? Nicely?

MHB: Yeah.

WW: What's Kim Porter getting for child support?

MHB: That's like a million-dollar question that I'd like to find out.

WW: That's the million-dollar question?

MHB: No one knows the exact number. There are things that you don't really know until you see it. I want to know.

WW: You'll never really know.

MHB: I know it's at least eight times what I'm getting. I do know that. At least.

WW: So it's in the five figures . . . monthly.

MHB: Yeah. Yeah.

WW: Do you have a life insurance policy?

MHB: Yes.

WW: It's not supposed to be like this [with the child support battle]. From my standpoint, as a gossip, you guys aren't supposed to be here. You're supposed to be able to work this out like Bruce and Demi.

MHB: Riiiight.

WW: If for no other reason than to save face for the public. Even if you get selfish and say, "Let's not think about Justin," think about saving face for the public. Diddy just ran the city for the kids, and he can't even get the shit together for his own kid? Give me a fucking break! Give me a break, Misa. That's not right. And he's got a mom who's alive who should be able to see him through to handle his baby's mother's situation correctly. Mother to mother, like you say to me.

MHB: (*Laughter.*)

WW: You know what I'm saying? You're the original baby's mother. You're the mother of Justin, the king of all restaurants. It's supposed to be better than this for you. I'm not saying he's supposed to be giving you money to luxuriate, because you have a husband and if I were him, I'd feel resentful, too and "Not a dime more, because she can get what she needs from him." But five thousand dollars a month? Isn't that Justin's security detail? I mean, gee.

MHB: I can tell you this much, the money he gives me, I could give *him* every month if it were the other way around. If he didn't work and was keeping Justin, I could give him the amount he gives me. That just shows how far back in money level it is.

WW: Why haven't you ever, ever said anything?

MHB: Publicly?

WW: To him!

MHB: I have.

WW: So what does he say to you?

MHB: No comment.

WW: Well, I have to tell you, this is not a good look for you two. I don't know what you've done in order to get him to talk to you, for it to get to this point. But it's my assessment of you, woman to woman, that you have done everything you could in keeping it quiet but letting him know, "Puff, I need more money." And he's obviously not been agreeable. So you have been forced to go public. He forced your hand. And you had to do what you had to do. That's very negligent on his part. That's very trifling. And it's a matter of public record so people will find out what's being paid, what has been paid, so on and so forth. Diddy can't run the city without him taking care of his own kids.

MHB: I won't say that he doesn't take care of his kids, because he does. But we haven't gotten our fair share.

WW: He went to check on the private schools—

MHB: I don't want to talk about any of that—

WW: Okay, fair enough.

MHB: This is the hardest thing that I've ever had to do. It's extremely hard. It hurts me, it bothers me.

WW: Is Justin getting talk back from friends at his school?

MHB: Justin knew about this when it started. He hears things and it's not anything new for him. He knows his dad loves him and that his mom loves him.

WW: And he's a wealthy little boy at the end of the day.

MHB: He's like me; that's just his life. He doesn't know any different. I don't raise my children as "rich" children. They have to clean up behind themselves. They have responsibilities. They have chores. They don't get everything they want. They have to get good grades on their report cards. They have to leave their homework out so I can check it and if it's not done well, they have to do it over. But when he goes with Puffy, he rides in private jets, he's on the yacht that Puffy rented, whatever big boat that was.

WW: Sounds scary for a kid. Sounds fabulous for me and you.

MHB: He also spends time with other family members who may live in Co-op City. He plays with kids. The only thing is we have to watch him. Someone always has to always be there.

WW: Kidnapping is really real.

MHB: Can't you just crack just thinking about that?

WW: Absolutely!

MHB: So that's the only thing that's really different. He has to be watched at all times. But sometimes he has people watching him and he doesn't know it. I don't want him to grow up feeling like "Where's my mom! Where's my dad? Where's security!" I want him to grow up confident and secure because he is the big brother.

WW: Right. Did you get along with Jennifer? Lopez?

MHB: Yeah.

WW: Did you ever style her or give her suggestions?

MHB: No. But she was really nice, though. She was nice to Justin. She was nice to me. She was really nice. If they were in Miami, I would go to Miami and bring Justin and drop him off and she would say, "You don't have to leave. You want to go swimming?" And I would say, "That's all right."

WW: I met her. I interviewed her. And she has—I don't like to think I'm being duped—but she has a very, very soft, pink side that I really appreciated.

MHB: *(Nodding in agreement.)* Mm-hmm.

WW: She'll make somebody a decent mother someday.

MHB: Yeah. She is really nice.

WW: Is she remotely in touch with Justin since the breakup? Will she send a card at holidays?

MHB: Uh-uh.

WW: Clean, as it should be. I was just asking.

MHB: She keeps in touch with Puffy's mom. And she has asked about me and how I was doing. From what I was told, she admired my independence. She thought nice things about me. People get from me and him that it's not still anything lingering there. It's like I'm a sister. An old relative or something. Or they feel comfortable. And the type of person I am, there's no bullshit with me. I'm pretty cut and dry.

WW: It makes it pretty safe that you have JoJo Brim. You're married and have your own thing going on.

MHB: And I don't carry myself like a slinky baby's mother, always around. I have my own life, my own things to do.

WW: Go on with your life with your burgundy Louis Vuitton bag and your burgundy hat. And P.S. from a stylist's point of view, I thought those were over, what do you say?

MHB: Maybe they are, but another interesting thing about me is that I don't go by what other people are doing. I like what I like. If I like something from last year, I wear it.

WW: Okay. Okay.

MHB: I'm a girly girl. I like my hat and I'm going to wear it. If they say blond hair is out and I feel like dyeing my hair blond, I'm going to dye it.

WW: Yeah, you had red for a long time.

MHB: I had black for a long time too. I do what I want. You too. Pink is not in style.

WW: I do love my pink.

MHB: It's funny. I was at the gym talking to this lady and she was looking at my nails. And she had burgundy nails. And she said, "I do this because it's the style now. I do the pink in the summer." And I was like, whatever.

WW: You seem to be a delightful woman. I don't make friends in this business. I try not to because I don't want to be caught out there, I want to be objective. But you are a very nice woman. It was nice talking to you.

MHB: It was nice talking to you too.

WW: Thank you, Misa. You are wonderful. I appreciate you coming.

MHB: The best thing about it is that it brings back so much history, so many memories.

10

The Dirty Backpack Clique

There is a movement in hip-hop—one where the artists are into a natural, holistic, clean way of life. Many of them are vegetarian or vegans. They believe in a higher being and are into their spirituality. They are throwbacks to a more mellow time in our history—they are hip-hop's version of the flower children.

I call them the dirty backpack clique. I imagine them with their dirty backpacks, filled with candles and incense, spiritual books, some nature bars, a few different kinds of herbs and oils. Most don't wear deodorant. And they don't drink hard liquor or take hard drugs. Marijuana is an herb, from nature, from God, so it is acceptable.

They are all about love, not war! India.Arie is the consummate dirty backpacker. She is the queen of the dirty backpack clique. She renamed her crew the Cosmic Citizens. And I accept that. And I believe India.Arie is a true cosmic citizen. She is my favorite cosmic citizen. I adore India.Arie. She is a wonderful woman. She has a beautiful spirit and a beautiful aura. I think she is genuine. And I really like that about her. She is in a class by herself.

But many of these dirty backpackers are hypocrites. They walk around talking about peace and love and the sisterhood and being all natural and being on a higher moral plane than everyone else, and they are the biggest offenders. They are the ones whose personal lives are in a shambles, who are rotten parents, and who morally need to check themselves. There are people who purport to live this lifestyle who beat their women and cheat on their men. And I'm not just talking about artists. There are everyday dirty backpackers, everyday people, who fall into this same category.

For women, if they answer yes to three or more of the following, they are officially part of this clique:

- Is your hair chemical free?
- Do you have more hair under your arms than on your head?
- When you put on a bathing suit, is there hair hanging out of the sides of your bottoms?
- Do you use Tom's toothpaste?
- Do you burn incense and avoid America's Next Top Model like the plague?
- Do you prefer Birkenstocks over stilettos?

These rules do not necessarily apply to those in entertainment, because the very nature of that business calls on people—women in particular—to put their backpack away and get beautiful from time to time. You cannot really stick to your dirty backpack convictions and expect to be wildly successful in Hollywood or even in music. You must wear makeup, put some polish on your nails, and wear some designer clothes and some pumps.

And while there are a few among the Hollywood backpackers who stick closely to their game—and I respect them for it—there are others who use it as a smoke screen. They are hypocrites who ride the dirty backpack mantra of being natural and real but whose lives are anything but natural and real.

There are those among the dirty backpackers who I deem to be judgmental and hypocritical. Lauryn Hill is one such dirty backpacker. When she came out with the *Miseducation of Lauryn Hill,* we were all pumping our fists for her messages of overcoming, shaking free from the bondage of her previous relationship with Wyclef, making her own path. She received eleven Grammy nominations. She won five Grammys, including Album of the Year and Best New Artist. She was the "it" girl of the late 1990s.

Lauryn Hill should actually be in the "Whatever happened to . . ." chapter. But I believe she still has enough going for her to snap out of it and mount a comeback. But when I think of Lauryn, I think how sad her situation is and how sad it is that she has fallen so far.

So what the fuck happened to Lauryn Hill and where is she now? Lauryn spazzed out on us, lost it, and now is completely off the radar. I think it's because all of that dirty-backpack, cosmic citizen shit was bullshit. Her whole image was built on a shaky foundation.

A problem that I have with Lauryn and people like her— many in the dirty backpack clique—is that they take a lot of pride in "keeping it real." They preach this all-natural lifestyle. They talk about "the people," and doing music and living a life to uplift the people. They talk about being natural and look down their noses on people with hair weaves, fake nails, and colored contact lenses.

Keeping it real? Really?

Some of them are into all of this spirituality stuff, yet they have no problem sleeping with another woman's husband. Now, what's that about? Or worse, some of them have no problem letting their man sleep with their cousin and have a child with that cousin. But people with hair weaves and fake nails aren't keeping it real? Pu-lease!

So Lauryn Hill presented herself as what society should aspire to with her realness, meanwhile she is cracking up before our very eyes and the girls with the fake boobs and fake contact lenses are probably better represented in society than she will ever be. Because what Lauryn represents is some weak-minded farce. Weak-minded because she allowed someone to take her mind and she is still out there and still hasn't managed to come back. Has anyone heard that last album of hers? Say no more.

There are many of these people who call themselves "all natural," who supposedly keep it real, whom I have put in a dirty backpack clique. They supposedly have all of these high morals and values, until you really check them out. There is nothing worse than a person who thinks they are better than you, based on some phony moral beliefs, and then you find out it's complete bullshit after all.

Lauryn is definitely a big disappointment. She had the biggest potential with all the Grammys, all the positive influence and leadership possibilities. And she just lost it. I must say that if your foundation is not strong, then you are going to crumble.

She did a big article for *Rolling Stone* a couple of years ago and said she would no longer be doing interviews for free. She now charges ten thousand dollars for an interview. I had managed to scrape together fourteen thousand dollars that I was going to give her for an interview. But I have decided that I don't really care to pay her for what she has to say anymore. She's irrelevant. I took that Lauryn Hill money and got my kitchen remodeled and I am very happy with that decision. A new kitchen made me much happier than listening to Lauryn Hill.

Erykah Badu is another dirty backpacker who is out there. Way out there. I have interviewed her a number of times. The last was in 2003, and each time she is nuttier and nuttier. Badu comes off like she's very concerned about family values. But isn't the very basis of family values holding down the man who planted the seed in you to have the baby? Am I wrong? Badu had the baby with Andre 3000 from OutKast. They never got married. They never even lived together as a family, the way I understand it. What kind of family values is she representing? And she's pregnant again. I don't know who the father is. But she's not married is she?

Wendy Williams (WW): Common said that he appreciated your spiritual connection that you make.

Erykah Badu (EB): He should.

WW: Evidently with your men, before you actually get with them.

EB: Right, Right. That's what I'm put on earth for.

WW: So Erykah Badu, in the studio everybody!

EB: That's right! Peace and love to everybody.

WW: Turn the music off, because I'm absolutely floored by this conversation right now.

EB: Peace and love, incense candles. [Badu snaps fingers.]

WW: *Okay, now you said you have three boyfriends—one of them is Common and the other two are both Dead Presidents?*

EB: *Yes, ma'am. That's how it works out. It's a new philosophy and we're trying to bring it to the United States. It's actually an African tradition from the Bambula tribe.*

WW: *Okay, now, Erykah, talk about this—once you're married, can you only have one husband?*

EB: *Well, there is no such thing as marriage in the Bambula tribe. It's just a way of life, the way we do it, the way we get down.*

WW: *All right. Very nice.*

EB: *None of this red, white, and blue thing, just red, black, and green all the way.*

WW: *Let me ask you this. What about Andre 3000?*

EB: *He's an honorary member right now. He tried to go through the course but he didn't get all the way.*

WW: *Well, apparently he did. You had the baby.*

EB: *Well, no, that doesn't mean anything. That's just procreation; that's what we're put on earth for. So it means nothing, really.*

And don't get me wrong, marriage isn't the end-all. But if you're going to have a child with someone and you say that family is important and you don't want to get married, then do it the way Kurt Russell and Goldie Hawn have done it. They have been together for more than twenty years. They have children and have never been married, but they are holding it down like a real family and I respect that. They represent for the life partners. And I respect life partners—whether they be hetero- or homosexual—as much as I do married partners, because despite it all, they are still a family and they honor commitment.

Badu couldn't hold down Dre and she couldn't hold it down with Common, and I'm not seeing her hold it down with this next baby's father. Commitment takes a certain level of maturity that Badu has not exhibited, as far as I'm concerned.

I first met Badu in 1997 before she came out with her debut album, *Baduizm*. One of her record label reps brought her to the studio. All she said was "Peace and blessings," and handed me an incense. I thought from that moment that she was strange. And over the years she hasn't done a single thing to change my initial opinion. She is stone-cold nuts.

Erykah Badu becomes an easy target because she was the first mainstream artist to introduce the dirty backpack clique. And she has made the biggest ass of herself—without my help. Her performance at the 2003 Lady of Soul Awards was classic. My parents were visiting me at the time and were watching the show. They had to call me to the television when she was on and asked me, "What's wrong with her?!" I had no response. She was onstage with a giant afro, gold caps on her teeth, and being completely incoherent. She was accepting an award and while I don't remember exactly what she said, I do recall the television folks cutting her off. It was very embarrassing to watch.

Now, she is someone my parents actually adored. They went to see her perform at Level Nightclub in Miami. They were in the front row and everything—two sixty-year-olds getting down. They stood the whole three hours, had weed passed to them (I believe they kept passing without puffing), and they even had water splashed on them by Badu. They had the best time, and Erykah said she remembers them. (I mean, how could you forget two sixty-year-olds in the front row of a concert?) But her recent antics made even my parents, two of her fans, scratch their heads.

Her 2003 interview on the *Experience*, I must say, was one of the strangest interviews I have done. What I was thinking throughout the interview was "What is she on?" I thought she was on something, because what type of a sense of humor must she have to think what she was doing was coming off as a joke?

She was saying some off-the-wall things:

> *WW: Okay, now, Erykah, talk about this—once you're married, can you only have one husband?*
>
> *EB: Well, there is no such thing as marriage in the Bambula tribe. It's just a way of life, the way we do it, the way we get down.*

and

> *WW: Okay, all right. When is the last time Andre and you had sex?*
>
> *EB: Umm ... I don't know. I don't remember the last time. I have an assistant that keeps a register of that. I would have to look through the records.*
>
> *WW: An assistant that keeps a register of when you have sex?*
>
> *EB: Yeah. With Andre.*

and

> *EB: Do I smoke weed? No. Well, actually, it's a new system that we use. It's not weed, it's a new herb that we found,*

found in the Himalayas by a young Chinese girl by
the name of CiCi Lywa. She brought it to the United
States and it's something that we use now. It's an herb
that we are trying to get cleared by the United States
board.

I did not have the strength to argue back and forth with her. I didn't have the strength to try and make sense of it all. I just chalked it up to Badu being Badu.

But one thing she said that I was most concerned about was that she had not gotten her son Seven vaccinated.

When she said she has not had her child vaccinated, I was floored. To me that was huge. I don't know what school admits a child these days without his or her vaccination records. You have to have proof from your pediatrician that all of the vaccinations are up-to-date and that your child is healthy. I understand living a natural life and all of that, but there are certain things that are just common sense and being a responsible parent. Why would any parent leave his or her child vulnerable to deadly diseases when they can be prevented through vaccinations?

And if he's homeschooled, well, okay, I guess. I just hope she's not the teacher. Her mother allegedly homeschooled her, and look how well that turned out. You figure the nut doesn't fall far from the tree. I'm not saying anything. I'm just commenting on someone not having a child vaccinated. And the sense (or lack thereof) of that.

WW: *Has Seven ever been vaccinated?*
EB: *No, ma'am. Never.*
WW: *So then he's not allowed to go to school?*

EB: *He's actually a special kind of baby.*

WW: *No, I mean school like the rest of us crazy people send our kids to.*

EB: *Why would we send him to that?*

WW: *I don't know; I'm trying to figure out why the rest of us nuts do that.*

EB: *No, we don't do that. That would mess him up.*

Lisa Bonet from *The Cosby Show* was the first celebrity I heard who was not vaccinating her child—the daughter she had with rocker Lenny Kravitz. It was the first time I had heard of such a thing. I wasn't a parent at the time, nor was I even thinking about having a child, but I thought it was a nutty thing to do even then. I didn't dwell on it because the whole children thing wasn't on my radar. But now that I am a mother and know what it takes to put your child in school and what it means to not have your child vaccinated, I wonder what kind of parents these "all natural" folks are.

Especially when you consider they are artists and spend a lot of time on the road and in other countries. Why would you want to leave your child open to all kinds of diseases that are found everywhere? I guess that means Erykah Badu doesn't get shots when she travels either. I guess she doesn't go to a gynecologist and get regular checkups. I guess she only takes herbs and stuff and that's good enough.

Badu or Lauryn, I don't know which one is more of a letdown. I say to them, "Look what you have become." Neither is a woman I would want some kid of mine to be looking at as a role model. They are both, in my opinion, nuts. I know that is such a cruel word, but it is apparently befitting both of them. Lauryn Hill had the potential to be an entertainer of the ages, someone we would be seeing ten, twenty years from now—still performing and still making a difference.

I don't see the same potential for Badu. Her act is wearing thin, quickly. I'm not saying that I'm a role model. But at least I'm really keeping it real!

11

Boob Jobs, Liposuction, and Rhinoplasty

For as long as I can remember, I have wanted to have a different body. My struggles with my body issues are well chronicled. I devoted an entire chapter to this subject in my last book. So when I finally had enough money to go to a plastic surgeon and pay cash for the work I wanted done, I did it. No hesitations, no fears. It's what I always wanted. Even when big girls, like Mo'Nique, who was a friend of mine at one time, were pumping their fists for the big girls and trying to make it okay for a woman to be big, I was always thinking, "You go with that! I'm getting liposuction, a tummy tuck, a boob job and the whole nine." And I did.

I'm one hundred percent pleased with every surgery that I have had. And when I turn sixty and my face is falling on the floor, I will get that lifted too. I believe in self-improvement. But I will caution that it is not for everyone. I will also caution that plastic surgery is very dangerous. There have been quite a few well-documented deaths on the operating table. Anesthesia can kill you. An infection can kill you. A botched surgery can kill you.

And death aside, don't look for plastic surgery to completely change your life. I got it because I always wanted it, but I never believed it would be a cure-all for anything wrong in my life. That was never my thought. I wanted to look better on the outside, but I was clear that if my insides weren't together, all the plastic surgery in the world wasn't going to fix that.

Too many people get plastic surgery thinking that it will bring them a man, a better job, success. I'm here to tell you that that's not true. Plastic surgery doesn't guarantee you anything—not even that you will end up beautiful afterward (and I will talk about a few bad plastic surgery jobs in this chapter). It definitely doesn't guarantee success. If beauty were all you needed, then explain why there are so many women who are born beautiful who aren't successful.

Plastic surgery is not something to enter into lightly. You have to do your research with doctors. If you're black, you have to make sure your surgeon knows how to deal with black skin, which heals and scars differently than white skin. There are plenty of white doctors who work well with black skin. My doctor is white. But you have to do your own research and ask lots of questions.

Just because a doctor is a plastic surgeon doesn't mean that he or she is good at all forms of plastic surgery. My doctor is a boob specialist, but if I were getting a nose job, I wouldn't necessarily want him doing it. If I were to get a nose job, I would prefer a black doctor. I find that oftentimes what is beautiful or nice looking to your doctor may not be right for your face. And if you do go to a white doctor, make sure you get before-and-after photos of the black patients he has operated on. I don't want to see an Indian or a Hispanic or a tanned white person. I want to see what you did with the black noses.

I have seen some pretty awful nose jobs on black people.

Singer George Benson's nose job is a mess. So is Peabo Bryson's. They must have gotten it done at the same place. I don't like Patti LaBelle's nose job either. But considering what she was working with originally, I guess that's the best they could do.

Stephanie Mills has a nice nose job, even though you can tell she had a nose job. Vivica A. Fox's nose looks cute at certain angles, but I hate to tell you that at other angles the bottom area of her nose needs work, because it looks like some kind of monkey nose in some pictures. And by the way, I don't think she's admitted to having a nose job, but as my listener Chanel in Long Beach, California, says, "surgery knows surgery." She listens every day. And she knows. I know too.

A really good nose job cannot be detected at first glance. You have to get the before-and-after photos and compare. Jennifer Lopez has a great nose job. She will deny that she has had a nose job, but check out her nose when she was a Fly Girl on *In Living Color* and look at her nose today. Halle Berry, in my opinion, also has had some work done, and I think it is tastefully done. I also think Mariah Carey has had some very nice and tasteful work done. But Mariah will deny all day that she has ever had *any* plastic surgery. Please, Mariah! I love you, but please! Check the before-and-after photos.

I know she had a boob job. The first time I asked her about it was when I interviewed her on the phone in Philly. She cursed me out and hung up on me. I tried to bring it up on three different occasions when we kissed and made up and she came to the studio in New York in 2003, and she evaded every reference.

WW: *And I asked you about your boobs and you got mad.*
MC: *Yeah, and I bought you a gift today. No, I didn't get mad, honey. But I brought you something.*

183

See, she changed the subject.

WW: *Now, what would this be? A push-up bra so I can have boobs like yours? I only have—*

MC: *Yes, no, no, no, no, no, no, no. You don't have this one, honey.*

She changed the subject again.

WW: *. . . and when I asked you about the boobs you cursed at me and hung up.*

MC: *No, no, no. I didn't curse at you and hang up. We joked, we had fun, and even your man over there . . . Where'd he go?*

And she changed the subject again. Mariah won't admit to it, but it looks to me that she has had more than a boob job. She looks to have had some chin work and liposuction too. "Surgery knows surgery."

I think hip-hop radio personality and rapper Ed Lover has had a nose job too. A listener pointed it out to me and I went to the before-and-afters and sure enough, he has. It is very well done. But I am conflicted about him getting it. He was on the radio in Los Angeles for a few years and was trying to really break into the acting game. And I guess in Hollywood everybody's getting work done. It's the land of perfection and plastic surgery. You're not part of the Hollywood scene unless you have gotten something done. And even if you haven't and you're a natural beauty, people still believe you did.

But Ed Lover? He's part of the hip-hop community first and I'm not comfortable with men in hip-hop getting plastic surgery. He's a black man from the hood, not a white man in Hollywood.

KRS-One has one of the largest noses I have ever seen. It's not only big, it's uniquely shaped. I almost give him permission to get a nose job. *Almost.* That nose is part of who KRS-One is. And he is, in my opinion, the essence of hip-hop—he keeps it real. He could never get a nose job. He's got to keep that nose; it's legendary.

Men in general, in my opinion, never have to get plastic surgery. Their imperfections are overlooked and even applauded. Look at Owen Wilson's hideously shaped nose. Yet he has managed to become a leading man. Men don't have to be gorgeous or even remotely fine to succeed in entertainment. I guess that's why I have such a negative reaction when I find out that a man has gone to such extremes as to have surgery to "fix" something. "Oh, my God, do you have feminine qualities or what?" I am thinking.

Rock-A-Fella rap mogul Damon Dash has had liposuction, according to his baby's mother and several other sources. I can't confirm it, but he has reportedly gone in several times for liposuction around his waist. And if he did get liposuction all I have to say is, "Lose the weight, dammit! Do the sit-ups, Dame!" There is something so vain about that.

I've embraced the whole metrosexualness of men. But I still have a problem going into a salon and sitting next to a man getting his nails or hair done. If I walk in and see that, I walk back out. I don't like it. And I do understand that a lot of men are getting manicures and just getting them buffed, but why do they have to do it in *my* nail salon? That's *our* spot. A nail salon to me is still very soft and pink. These men need to find their own place to get their nails done.

I also hate it when people get plastic surgery and totally forget who the hell they are. I believe this happened to Lil' Kim. Lil'

Kim was hard core, hood-representing, just raw with it. She was hood hot. But somewhere along the way, Lil' Kim lost her gangsta.

A couple of things happened to change her. First, Biggie died. After he died and she was left to her own devices, her music wasn't turning out with the same kind of heat and her rap career was going south. Then she got bit by the Hollywood bug.

All of a sudden she started getting invited to the fashion shows. Kim's got a great personality. She's a sweet, sweet girl and I can imagine her charming the pants off of the big-time designers like Michael Kors and Roberto Cavalli and white Hollywood. She's very charming.

The next thing you know, she's on the cover of mainstream magazines and partying at mainstream events. Perhaps she felt she had to now fit in with this mainstream crowd. But I guess she forgot that this crowd was hanging out with her because she was Lil' Kim—hard-core, hood-representing, raw Lil' Kim.

It started innocuously with implants and, I believe, a little liposuction. Then she got her teeth capped, which seems harmless. But I asked my dentist about getting some of those porcelain veneers and he told me that it's really only for people with really jacked-up teeth. What they do is file down your own teeth to little black points (the teeth turn black after the roots are exposed) and then they place the veneers over that. That's extreme, especially for someone like Kim, whose own teeth were just fine.

And then came the nose job, and that's when I said that she went too far. Her nose job didn't turn out well at all either.

Part of my problem with Lil' Kim's nose job—aside from the fact that it's hideous—is that there is a bit of sellout in it.

I grew up in predominantly white Ocean Township, New Jersey where, for many of the girls, a nose job was almost like a rite of passage. "Happy thirteenth birthday, here's your nose job." We never thought twice about it, it was that accepted.

There is a huge difference in the black community, however. Plastic surgery is not something that "we" do. In fact, there are a lot of things "we" don't do in the black community—enter rehab, seek marriage counseling, take care of our diets. We eat a lot of artery-clogging, stroke-threatening food because it's the way we've always eaten—which is why there is such a high risk of high blood pressure, heart attack, and stroke among blacks. And when I go to Bally's, I would like to see more black people in there working out too. I believe that eating correctly and exercise are keys to staying healthy. This is something I have grown into later in life, but I firmly believe in it. But it's not something, by and large, that "we" do.

But despite the stigma, I firmly believe in plastic surgery. As I mentioned before, plastic surgery should only come *after* you are solid within yourself. I pump my fists for people who try to improve themselves any way they can. But I am troubled when I see, like in the case of Lil' Kim, people are getting all of this work done on the outside when the real job needs to be done on the inside.

Kim started out as a black girl from the hood and now she's posing as a white girl from Hollywood. It's not a good look for Kim. And I believe it has hurt her career. She has lost her credibility with her core base of fans. And it's not just because she's had plastic surgery, it's because she's lost her identity.

Mary J. Blige has allegedly gotten breast implants, but there is still something very real about her. Mary still has the respect.

Kim didn't just get a nose job, she got a head job. Kim even speaks a different way when she's in white company than she does when she's in black company. And that's not keeping it real.

So if you're going to get plastic surgery, make sure you know who you are and that you're getting it for the right reasons.

CHAPTER

12

How You Doin'?

The music industry is run by homosexuals. Top to bottom, everybody from the interns to the executives, homosexuals can be found in the music industry.

People ask me what's the fastest way to get down? As I mentioned in *Wendy's Got the Heat,* the fastest way to get down is to get down. And if the record label executive is gay and you happen to be of the same sex, you can always be homosexual or lesbianic with someone and get ahead. Hell, the women that are making things happen in the business, hmm. I'm not saying anything, I'm just saying, hmm.

The fashion industry, the music industry, from top to bottom are very gay friendly. If you're a participant, that's the better choice. And when we talk about hip-hop and you want to know why it is so prevalent, it is because there are a lot of people who have a dream of making it in that business. They have no aspirations of going to college or working in a trade. Maybe they're not as pretty as a Kim Porter and can't Baby's Mama their way to success. Or maybe they're not handsome enough, like a Tyson Beckford, and can't model their way to the top.

But they need to get out of their situation, they want out of their poverty, and are willing to do anything, *anything,* to get out—even if it means having sex with someone of the same sex. And if they're marginally talented, they can make it. Marginal talent can be fixed up in a major way in the studio. Look at Jennifer Lopez. Look at Ashanti.

Bigger than talent is cooperation with the honchos, and one of the biggest forms of cooperation is sex. And just because you're a pretty woman—and, yes, guys are going to ask you to have sex—don't think you won't get approached by a female executive as well.

I got into this industry as a professional in 1987. I did not come home—to the music I enjoyed listening to—until 1990, when I was hired at 98.7 KISS. Prior to that, I had worked at stations that featured oldies and Top 40, and I wasn't paying attention to these artists. I wasn't going to the parties and I wasn't listening to their music, I was just doing my shift. In 1990 when I got my job at KISS, all of a sudden I am going to the parties and seeing the stars of that time. I am seeing the top acts of that time and the top moguls. And there I am.

I may be an outsider because I am the bigmouth gossip from the radio, but I am still at the parties watching and observing. And some of the things I was seeing, all I could say was, "Oh, my gosh! It's homo crazy in here!"

The first rapper that I can clearly say that I met and I was like "Oh, my, what a homo!" is a platinum artist today. And I can't say his name, but I can tell you that he has been in the game a long time. When I first met him, he came up with his group. He's from the tristate area and he was the ringleader of this group. They had a few hits in the early 1990s and the group has since broken up. They're all broke, basically, except for the ringleader, who went on to enjoy platinum status, hanging with the likes of Mariah Carey and even endorsing a few mainstream products.

White people love him and so does the urban community. But he can't really go into his old neighborhood without getting robbed because his secret is falling out of the closet so fast.

I used to work with a singer whose career flopped and she became a radio disc jockey. We were friendly and she used to screw around with this rapper. She told me that he used to always want anal sex from her. She finally came to me and asked, "Wendy, is he gay?" And I said, "Hmm, I was waiting for you to finally ask me." I would never say anything unless asked. But when she asked I said, "Yes, honey, he is as gay as the day is long."

He was straight-up trying to be hard for the public, when the truth was he was anything but. I first met him with his group around 1991. They came up to the studio and before the interview, the other guys left to go to the lobby or the bathroom or something and he stayed behind in the studio with me. We had a wonderful time. He kept calling me "girlfriend" and we sat and chatted like old, well, girlfriends, if you know what I mean.

He was not hitting on me at all, but we were vibing in that way—in the way a gay man vibes with a woman. And I thought, "I love it! He's so hard but so soft. Look how his demeanor has changed from his on-air persona. Wow!"

He went on to be a breakout star. He has a beautiful personality. Early on, before he became a breakout star, we used to see each other at parties and he might give me the two-cheek kiss, step back, and say, "Girlllll, you look fabulous!"

I believe we could have been very friendly, but he had a secret. And back then so did I. You know, I had a cocaine habit and

I wasn't interested in being anybody's friend. But since I wrote my book, I have now found out that everybody was skied up back then.

While I was busy hiding in the bathroom, little did I know I probably could have sprawled my stuff out on the console in the studio and had one big party. Everybody seemed to be involved in that kind of activity. But I didn't know. I kept to myself. So I didn't make many friends.

And today this rapper and I are not only *not* friendly but we don't really talk, I think he thinks, because I know his secret, I'm going to blow him up. But in actuality, I wouldn't blow him up. That's old Wendy, which is why I'm not saying his name right now. I may throw a few *"How You Doin's?"* out there when talking about him on the radio show. But if it came up, I would never put him on blast.

I remember thinking back then that he was so cool. This guy who was so tough on the mic but was so girlfriendy behind the scenes. It's a shame he has to hide who he really is. He has kids. He's successful. And he's gay.

There's another major rapper from New York who is in the same category. He, too, was part of a group and he branched off to become a big solo artist. This rapper's name, in my opinion, is synonymous with *homosexual.* I have interviewed him several times on my show and one time even with his lover, who is also a rapper whose name you would know instantly. The rapper is married. His lover is not married. The lover is the only one allowed to call his house any time of day or night.

How do I know they are lovers? If for proof I need to be in the hotel room and see them in the throes of passion, then I don't know. But trust me when I tell you, they have the connection. You can see it. It's blatant.

They are good friends. But they are friends with benefits. I just learned that phrase last year. One of my listeners called up for advice and said she was married but she has a friend with benefits outside of her marriage. And I asked her, "Are you that hard up for health insurance?!" But another listener explained to me that a "friend with benefits" meant a friend that you have sex with. Ohhhhhh! So this rapper has a good friend with benefits.

This rapper's wife has called me twice in the last year, agonizing over his sexuality. She has the hotline number directly into the studio. The old Wendy would have put her on the air immediately. But I am so long in the tooth now that I don't feel the need to put every damn body who has a scandal on the radio. Sometimes I just say to my producer, Art, and Dave, my engineer, "Play another song while I talk to this woman in the other room." And the story is sad. But not unique.

These girls meet these rappers and singers and actors—because it goes across the board and cuts along racial lines too—under a haze. These guys are famous and rich. Maybe there is weed and champagne or worse. The girls are young, maybe eighteen, when they meet. And by the time they get married they have been exposed to so much wealth, showered in so many diamonds, living the high life, that they aren't thinking about perhaps he's gay.

And this particular rapper is huge—a platinum-selling artist with his group and solo. These girls get used to a certain lifestyle. They're not hanging out with regular people like me and you. There are usually their homegirls from back in the day and they shop at Gucci and Louis. Nobody's observing the whole homo aspect. People take any flamboyancy as "Oh, that's entertainment!" Any late-night hour or thug boys hanging around is "Oh, that's just the industry," or "That's part of the business."

And gayness is very much part of the industry and part of the business. World talked about it on a level few people have the courage to do. And so did Suge Knight. The first time I interviewed him we talked about the topic. I won't repeat anything from our interviews because I don't want to be sued, but if you want to hear what World and Suge had to say, blow by blow, I will make it available to purchase. Neither one of them holds back and they really give a perspective on this gay thing that I think is important—especially for women who are in the most danger of either catching a disease or getting emotionally hurt in a relationship with one of these men.

Let me tell you, every woman needs gaydar. It is your best friend. You develop gaydar by living and observing. You do not develop gaydar by staying in your house. You can have sharpened gaydar by age twenty-five easy, but you have to get out and watch and observe the scene.

You have to keep in mind that just because a particular man is a straight-up thug or a married banker doesn't mean he can't be gay. On the other hand, you have to keep in mind that just because a man is good at picking out a nice dress for you, hates sports, and is good at decorating the house or cooking doesn't mean that he is gay. It is such a fine line and you just really have to know it.

I love a gay man, by the way—just not as a husband. That's not what I was looking for. I don't particularly love a gay man as a father unless it's part of the plan as a stick-and-move. If you're just trying to land him and you don't care if he's gay and he has money and you're just trying to be taken care of—that's a plan. But know what you're getting yourself into before you do that. Know what you're dealing with.

I am asked all the time how to know if your man is gay. My best advice is watch his friends. What you might think are just guys hanging out, one of his best boys could be his lover. Hell, it could be a whole circle of them. And out of his friends, there will always be that one who will give you the swooshy tip-off. It doesn't mean that your man is gay or on the down-low, but watch his friends. I didn't say accuse anybody, just watch his friends.

I would say watch your man's mannerisms, but contrary to popular belief there is not one stereotype for anyone—not for black people, not for Italians, not for gay people. So looking for the usual suspect behavior may not work.

But if you really want to know where to find a large number of secret homosexuals, look no further than the music business. It's something I have been talking about for years, but it wasn't until 2004 when I sat down with World that everything was put into perspective for me.

World is a guy, not famous in the game of music, not a charting, platinum rapper. But he is an insider. He was once the boyfriend of Lil' Kim. He contacted me to come do an interview about what I thought would be some dish on Lil' Kim. Some of my best interviews come from disgruntled exes. But what he ended up talking about, many of my listeners are still buzzing about. He basically blew the doors off of hip-hop, describing it as a secret society of homosexuals.

The things he had to say were so explosive that we taped the interview a day beforehand. A live interview, in my opinion, would have put him in jeopardy of anyone rolling up to the studio and waiting for him afterward.

Before he came to meet with me, I knew of World by reputation. World and Lil' Kim were together less than a year but during that short period, he completely controlled the situation and had Lil' Kim on lockdown. He determined what she would do and who she would talk to. And during his time with her, the *Experience* was off limits for Lil' Kim. Part of me understood the relationship. I, too, have a man in my life who is running my career. But there was another part that wasn't feeling this World character.

I heard interesting things about World that were not so nice pertaining to his street game. He apparently was good at threats and intimidation. People were afraid of World—much the way they are afraid of Suge Knight. And I pictured him in my mind to be this big, strapping, scary-looking dude.

When I saw him I was like "Wow! This is the world-famous World." He was slightly built—shorter and smaller than I am—soft-spoken and handsome.

But he's still dangerous. Another kind of dangerous. And he is fearless. I was the one who suggested the taping of the show, because I understood the peril he was placing himself in by saying the things he said during our interview. But he wasn't worried. He is also a practicing Muslim. And he had his Koran with him during the interview and was open about his beliefs.

I found World to be very credible, although some of his claims were hard for me to swallow—like the Masons and their link to this secret society of homosexuals. I know too many Masons, and this one I do not buy at all. But World believed everything he said. He spoke with great conviction. I found World easy to talk to, even though parts of the interview were like deciphering hieroglyphic codes from the Egyptian tombs.

That interview is one of my most requested reruns. I haven't replayed it because I had planned on putting the entire transcript in this book. I wanted people to read for themselves, but it's so over the top that the editors got nervous. So I just took snippets.

World: *All right now, you got a lot of these cats, if you hear them in they rhymes, a lot of them is spitting the language and they're really nothing but puppets for the bigger people. And, you know, everybody knows that, everybody knows about these people but everybody scared to speak up.*

WW: *Well, I want you to speak and I want you to tell me, because right now we're talking a secret language.*

World: *All right, let's, I'm, I'm, I'm, no, no, I'm letting, I'm getting ready to jump deep into it.*

WW: *Okay.*

World: *All right now, in that little circle, they, you all know that, um, you have to be sworn to secrecy.*

WW: *Yes.*

World: *So it depends on what type of level you in this thing to whereas how you have to be sworn to secrecy.*

WW: *Got you.*

World: *These rappers, they know how to, they gotta be sworn to secrecy by homosexuality. . . . But okay, listen, listen. Only thing you have to do is pay attention to the way these dudes look.*

WW: *Okay.*

World: *These dudes are grown men. How you running around in all these videos and all that and you ain't got no facial hair? That's because they imitating the people that built the pyramids. If you look at them dudes throwing up the Dynasty sign . . .*

WW: *Okay.*

World: Yeah, this is, this is what these dudes represent, but they really don't know what they following. They're really, really lost. Like the devil is really fooling these people. They really don't understand what they following. They're just soldiers and puppets for the bigger people. And if you pay attention to what's going on, like they're really trying to step in, into the Muslim world with their music and all that. You see these dudes now in videos all in deserts and all that. On camels and stuff, you understand?

WW: Yes. What's wrong with women? I mean, what are we, lepers?

World: What do you mean?

WW: I don't understand. What do you think comes first? The urge to be down or the joining the organization and finding out what you have to do to be down?

World: This is what it is.

WW: What?

World: A lot of these dudes they just want, they want a few dollars.

WW: Right?

World: So, they don't really understand what's going on.

WW: Right.

World: A lot of them right now, wish that they couldn't, wish that they didn't have to go that way.

WW: World is in the studio, everybody! I believe that too. I've always said, there are [those who are] born and then you're down and then there are others who are turned out for things—whether it's money or fame or whatever.

World: Exactly!

WW: And I, they're, um . . .

*World: All right, we can, let's look at it like this ... They got
dudes faking they deaths and all kinds of things. Like
this is really crazy. All right, let's look at the history of
these people.*

A lot of people thought that World was a crackpot and were
wondering why I wasted time talking to him. But I realized that
people don't like to think any deeper than required. While World
was saying some crazy things, he was also saying some things to
make you think. And on my radio show I can interview anyone
from the latest rapper that is so new we don't know anything
about him all the way to Russell Simmons to someone like World.

I don't like to pigeonhole myself where all I interview are
celebrities. World was not a celebrity. He was a guy who used to
date Lil' Kim, who had some insight on the music business and
on life that he wanted to share with the people. And I gave him
a platform to share it. And ultimately, I did so as a public service.
There are a lot of dealings going on in the world of music and a
lot of young people dying to get into the game. They need to
know what they're looking at. They need all the information
they can get their hands on.

CHAPTER

13

Whitney Houston

My interview with Whitney Houston took place on December 15, 2002, two weeks after her big sit-down with Diane Sawyer on ABC *Primetime.* During Whitney's interview with Diane Sawyer it was clear to me (and anyone who watched it, for that matter) that Whitney was in a bad way . . . and you fill in the blanks.

Diane Sawyer—who defined herself as the premier interviewer of our times—registered for the first time on my radar with that interview. I was more shocked at the *gangsta* that Diane Sawyer showed than the responses that Whitney gave to her questions. Diane Sawyer skillfully backed Whitney into an uncomfortable corner and she had Whitney up against several times. So I wasn't surprised by anything that Whitney was saying because her interviewer put her in a position where she had to answer the questions. And I was sitting there rooting for Diane Sawyer. I was rooting for her.

Two of the most memorable statements to come out of that interview were Whitney's responses to Diane's questions about her drug use. Whitney said, "I don't use crack because crack is whack!" and "You show me the receipts!" And while it was sad to watch, it was also one of the more humorous moments in television history. For days and weeks following the interview people could be heard commenting and laughing about those two statements. In fact, I had a listener of the *Experience* fax me in receipts from places like Target that read: "Paper Plates: $.99, body lotion: $3.99, cocaine: $250 . . ."

It would be truly funny, if it wasn't so sad.

Whitney's behavior was frightening and her body language was very telling. I might have cut plenty of classes at Northeastern, but one class that I excelled in was Body Language 101. And she was a classic case study in deception. Whitney held on to the white pillow on her couch in that Diane Sawyer interview for what looked like dear life. She was perspiring and frequently touching her face, which, body language experts will tell you, indicates deception.

The appearance of Bobby Brown was absolutely telling. And when she brought on Bobbi Kristina I had one hand on the telephone to call child services.

One week after the interview, my husband, son (who was two at the time), and I went to see Whitney Houston perform live at Lincoln Center, which was going to be aired on *Good Morning America*. It was very, very cold, but we braved the elements because I had to see for myself, I had to see her in person.

She was wearing jeans, a white turtleneck, camel coat, and a short wig. And she performed brilliantly, considering what I had been expecting. She had a problem getting through one song, but for the most part she was, vocally, the Whitney that many of us have grown to love. Hell, when you have a voice as beautiful as

Whitney's, you can lose a bit of the magic and still outsing most of the chicks out there.

That day, I noticed two things. One, perhaps she had lost a little bit of her magic, but that could be easily explained away. It was very cold. Two, I noticed the enthusiasm of the crowd—estimated at more than three thousand people, young and old, black and white—and I knew that the moment Whitney cleaned up her act, people would be right back in her corner, supporting her.

While there were those who showed up that particular day to stare at Whitney and look for the telltale signs of her perhaps being high, there were others, many others, to stare in awe, rocking to the music and singing the words to her songs.

Which one was I, you ask? I was neither. I was there with a two-year-old who prevented me from doing much else than pay attention to him. I left there thinking I was glad Whitney had done the concert and it appeared that she was on a mission of damage control. She had to make the rounds to show the world that she was okay. But she was clearly not okay.

I got the call the following week that Whitney Houston was coming on my radio show, the *Experience,* on WBLS in New York City. I was surprised, but not really. I figured she had to "make good" for that Diane Sawyer interview, and what better place than the *Experience*? ☺

But I wasn't going to hold my breath. One thing that I've learned is that you can't trust a substance abuser to be reliable. Now, I'm not saying that Whitney is a substance abuser, but I was. And fingers have been pointed at her. At the very least she has a long track record of being unreliable in terms of not showing up for concerts and other appearances. So what makes my radio show so important that she will follow through and call? Besides, ultimately, she's an artist and artists have a habit of not following up on appointments.

So when my manager (who also happens to be my husband, Kevin) called and told me that Whitney Houston would be calling in twenty minutes, I didn't miss a beat. I kept right on with my show and never said a word to my audience. I figured if she called, great. If she didn't, no loss.

Actually, I don't make a habit of letting people know who is coming to visit my show before they arrive. Too often people have gotten talked out of coming when their friends or record labels hear they are on their way to visit me. I get a lot of celebrities who come up to the show on their own and after the interview their record label will say, "Why the hell did you do that?! We set up your interviews and you were to avoid her show!"

I've been called a publicist's worst nightmare. So I wasn't preparing for Whitney. Besides, if you have to prepare questions for Whitney Houston, you're not much of a pro. To my surprise, Whitney Houston did call. She called about five o'clock, with one hour remaining on my show. I popped in a DAT, which I use to record all of my interviews, and told my producer to play music while I interviewed Whitney behind the scenes.

I normally interview everyone live, but this time I had a feeling going to tape would work better. Sometimes a guest knows if they curse or act really ill that it can end an interview prematurely. That happened to me in Philadelphia in 2000 when I was interviewing Mariah Carey. I slipped in a question about her breasts saying, "Wow, Mariah, your implants look great!" And she shot back, "I don't have any fucking implants, Wendy. So put that on the gotdamn radio. Shit!" And it was on the radio . . . end of interview. I wasn't taking any chances with Whitney Houston. If she wanted to curse and act ill, she could do it to her heart's content and we would just edit all of the cursing out and play it all for the people.

I had never interviewed Whitney Houston, but I knew she was prone to cursing. In fact, I had never met her before. But I knew she knew me. I had been talking about Whitney Houston on my radio show since she married Bobby Brown. She's provided enough material to keep me in business for years—from declaring Bobby Brown to be the original king of R & B to her missing appearances and sweating like a pig on awards shows to her relationship with Robin to her breast implants to her pregnancy and eighty-pound weight gain to her near-skeletal appearance on the Michael Jackson special. Whitney has always had a great behind-the-scenes life that has provided more than enough grist for the mill. So I looked at this interview as yet another chapter.

The decline of Whitney Houston—perhaps the greatest diva of our times—is the biggest scandal of this generation. It is bigger than that Michael Jackson mess. Bigger than Kobe Bryant. Bigger than Diana Ross. Bigger than Ben and Jen. Bigger than Robert Blake and O. J. Bigger than Janet Jackson's boob. In my opinion, the downfall of Whitney Houston is so huge because we have witnessed her literally implode right before our eyes. We have watched her go from our princess, a role model, a gracious woman, to what looks to be one step above a crackhead. For me, as a fan, it's just really sad, because events don't seem to be headed toward a happy ending. I pray that they are, but the signs aren't good.

I thought the Diane Sawyer interview would be a wake-up call for Whitney—a catalyst to her getting it together. Then she comes on the *Experience* and takes it to a new low. And after that interview, the madness didn't stop in her world. In May of 2003 Whitney and Bobby went to Dimona, Israel, as guests of the black Hebrews. They were there on some sort of pilgrimage, a spiritual journey, with both Whitney and Bobby getting baptized in the river Jordan. Whitney, who had admitted that she used drugs, had said that she didn't need rehab. All she needed was Jesus. But Jesus can't help you if you're not going to cooperate. So that trip to Israel ended up a fiasco, with Whitney acting very strange. She even refused to shake the hand of Israel's prime minister Ariel Sharon and was seen just acting weird.

When they returned from Israel, they were back to their old tricks. Not more than a month after coming back, Whitney showed up late for her own birthday party, sparking debate again about whether or not she was using. Then, later in August of 2003, Whitney and Bobby were back in the news when Bobby was arrested and sentenced to fourteen days in jail and sixty days of house arrest for probation violation.

In December of 2003, Whitney called 911 following a fight with Bobby. The cops arrived to find a disheveled Whitney with a cut lip and bruised cheek. Bobby was nowhere to be found. He turned himself in days later and there was Whitney, standing by her man. They left the court all kissy-kissy, acting like everything was fine. Everything is clearly not fine in that household.

This incident wasn't the first time I had heard about Bobby Brown hitting Whitney. I wasn't surprised by it. Whitney's whole journey has turned into such an unbelievable and some-times comical, yet sad, story that nothing that I hear about her surprises me. And I tend to believe the things I hear more often than not.

My opinion on why Whitney does some of the things she does—pumping her fist for Bobby after leaving the courthouse and jumping into his lap and all of that—is that the amount of money Whitney has amassed probably gives her the feeling that she can do what she wants. She doesn't seem to care what anyone thinks about her.

If she wants to buy a brick of coke and stay in the house and do that brick of coke all day, she can do that and still have more money than all of us. Her bills are still being paid on time. She's doing it with her husband, it's not like she's out cheating on her husband. She's not necessarily doing it around her daughter. They have a big enough house and they have houses in other states.

I wasn't shocked when the story came down in March 2004 that Whitney had checked herself into a rehab center. The day that I found out was the same day that the New York *Daily News* ran a piece in the gossip pages about Star Jones and her fiancé, Al Reynolds, questioning his sexuality. That, honestly, was a bigger topic of conversation with my girlfriends later that day. Some of my girlfriends who are single and would love to be married were criticizing Star for being with a man who used to (or perhaps still does) play for the other team. But I was defending Star. Hell, she knew full well what she was getting into. That's her business. But that's what we wanted to talk about. The story of rehab and Whitney was just a passing sentence in our conversation.

When I heard about it, and it's terrible to say because I am an ex-offender who has overcome, I rolled my eyes and said, "Okay, we'll see if it works." My next question was "Who pushed her into it?" I didn't see this as a move Whitney made on her own.

The next question I had was "Why did she wait until two weeks before Bobby was getting out of jail?" Why would she check in with his release time so close? By the time she got out, there his ass would be waiting for her. And then what? She would be at a much different place, but for how long?

I don't see Bobby going to rehab too. Men aren't much for seeking help. And black men? Forget about it. Black women are just now coming around. We used to just take all our problems to the Lord and to church. Now some of us are getting real counseling for our problems. Not that church can't help, but sometimes you need professional help.

I hope rehab works out for Whitney. But I'm not optimistic, especially if she was forced or threatened into it by her family. If you're dragged off and your heart's not in it, you have less of a chance to succeed. You have to want to quit. I know. And coming back to that same home, back to that same man, back to that same life, will certainly drive her back to the drugs. Guaranteed.

If I were Whitney, I would sell the house. Hell, I would move to another state. I would fire everyone who had worked for me in the past—anyone who had ever seen me high would have to go—every maid, every butler, every hairstylist, every clothing stylist.

Speaking as a sober woman, I know how important it is to clean house totally. You can acknowledge in yourself all of the things you've done, but you don't need people around who remind you of those things. Their mere presence can be enough to remind you of when you were falling down high and they helped you take your pants off to go to the bathroom. Those are the kinds of things that can send you back there.

I would get rid of everybody except the daughter and perhaps her mother.

Yes, she should get rid of Bobby too. He is a drunkard, a druggie, a criminal, an abuser, a philanderer, half a father, half a husband, and has no income. What?! Get rid of him!

Move from New Jersey and start a whole new life. She's forty now and it's time to start fresh—that's what being forty is all about. She's no longer a pop star. I'm sure that Whitney has reckoned with the fact that she may never be that pop star again. But this isn't about the music for Whitney Houston anymore, this is about survival. This is about her life. The last thing we want to see her end up as is another Billie Holiday.

I pray that Whitney comes out of rehab clean and that she stays clean. I pray that Bobby gets help too. I would love to see Whitney and Bobby be clean together. They will still be that tumultuous couple. Because even without drugs they both still have fire in them.

I have to admit, I cannot get enough of Whitney and Bobby. They make my job easy. And interviewing her was the crowning jewel of my career. I very much enjoyed that interview. I was shocked by some of the things she said and the way she expressed herself, but I was pleased with the way it went.

There were people—and I will say it wasn't the majority—who thought that Whitney got the best of me during that interview. But those are people who really don't understand that I knew exactly what I was doing. From the moment Whitney got on the phone, she sounded very high to me. And as a person who used to get high, I would know. So I knew it was going to be very entertaining, because she was going to be doing all of this chatting. And even if she hung up on me—which I completely expected at some point—that, too, would be entertaining. I had nothing to lose.

The reason why I didn't respond to many of the things she was saying was because what would be the point? There was no rationalizing with Whitney. Why should I come back at her and try to reason with someone who seemed high to me? So, I took . . . the high road—no pun intended.

And the result: One of the best Whitney Houston interviews of all time. VH1 named the following interview one of the network's top hundred moments.

INTERVIEW SESSION
Whitney Houston

WH: Wendy, Wendy, Wendy.

WW: Oh, my, gosh.

WH: Oh, my lord, have I waited for this day.

WW: Have you?

WH: Well, yes, I have . . . haven't you?

WW: Whitney?

WH: Yes, dear?

WW: Absolutely!

WH: I know it.

WW: I don't believe that I ever met you in my entire career.

WH: Ain't that funny? You talk about me all the time.

WW: And you *are* top billing.

WH: Is that why you talk about me all the time?

WW: Absolutely.

WH: 'Cause, you never even met me; you don't even know me!

WW: But, here's the thing. I talk about you in two ways. In the way that the media talks about Whitney—

WH: Yup.

WW: —but I always talk about you as being one of the greatest voices of our time. Mariah Carey is another one. You two do two separate works, but you have a voice that is just . . . unbeatable, Whitney.

WH: I love you, Wendy, and I thank you for that. I really do. 'Cause I know that in spite of everything, you play my records.

WW: I do.

WH: I know that.

WW: And I also feel that you and I have something in common.

WH: We do!?

WW: Umm . . . well, yeah. Besides, besides the, you know, the motherhood thing and—

WH: Okay.

WW: —and so on and so forth. Whitney, your new CD is out now.

WH: Yes.

WW: The first week it did very well. It's not doing quite as well right now . . . compared to perhaps what the record label thought it would be doing.

WH: Well, it's never what you thought I should be doing.

WW: Okay.

WH: It's never what you think I should be doing. It's never what you think, you *say* I'm doing. It is what's going to happen. You see what I'm saying? I don't want my album to peak too quickly; I don't want it to peak too quickly. I don't want it to peak too quickly because I want it to go through the summer.

WW: Aha.

WH: And through the fall.

WW: Aha. Okay, I understand.

WH: So there is a plan.

WW: Okay.

WH: You understand what I mean? Like you set up a schedule on a day-to-day basis, on who you're gonna talk about and how you're gonna talk about them.

WW: Yes.

WH: Well, that's how I do.

WW: So we play; we love the song the "Dear John Letter" here on the show.

WH: Yes, ma'am.

WW: And, umm . . . speaking of letters, you no longer have to write to Bobby. Bobby is out of jail. Bobby's back home now?

WH: Yes, baby. You ain't . . . you get all the info don't you? You got the four one one, you should know.

WW: I want to make sure that I have all my stories straight.

WH: Haahaaaa!

WW: Mmm-hmm! (*Laugh.*)

WH: Yes, baby, he's home, well and intact.

WW: Do you regret the Diane Sawyer interview?

WH: No. Why should I?

WW: Well, it didn't exactly show you in the best light.

WH: No? You don't think so. Well, you know, Wendy, you don't show yourself in the best light and people still listen to you.

WW: Yeah, but I'm on the radio every day . . .

WH: Yeah, well, we just don't get to see your face, but they should know what *you look* like.

WW: I understand that, Whitney, perhaps one day I will have a TV show. But in terms of what I do—

WH: Yeah?

WW: When I'm not shown in the best light—

WH: Mm-hmm.

WW: —I guess one of the best things that I love about my career is that there's always tomorrow to come back.

WH: And see, and what I love about my career—

WW: Aha?

WH: —is that my music speaks for itself.

WW: Yeah, well, it does.

WH: Ya know what I mean. So I mean, I am the second most watched interview behind Monica Lewinsky in the history of interviews.

WW: I'm surprised you're second to her. I mean as far as—

WH: I mean. Ya know, I'm not like too cool about coming behind her, but, ya know, it's all right with me because, umm, ya

know . . . I got a lot of mileage, some that I think the people basically . . . the people that I talk to that'll make comments to me—

WW: Aha?

WH: —were very proud of me. Because it was a moment . . .
See, I'm not one for sitting down and talking to people. I,
ya know . . . you can talk all you want about me, but my
mother always said don't try to dignify the lie with truth. Ya
know, because then you make it worse. Because people
like to lie . . . for whatever reason they like to lie on you,
about you.

WW: Right.

WH: However, umm . . . I thought that it was a major step for me
to sit with Diane Sawyer, the biggest interviewer in the
world, and talk with her, and give her what . . . umm, basically, umm, I thought I could give. Ya know, and I think
people enjoyed that, seeing me. And seeing, umm . . . me
growing and being a spiritual person, and that I have a
family that loves me and cares about me and—

WW: Well, yeah. No, it was very entertaining

WH: You thought it was entertaining?

WW: Yes.

WH: Ahhhh, you're funny!

WW: Yeah. I mean, please. Me and everybody, we were all
watching together. I recently—

WH: There were some very funny moments.

WW: Yeah, yeah. From start to end it was quite entertaining,
Whitney.

WH: Well, I'm glad you were entertained. Because you watched
it, didn't you?

WW: So, Whitney, as far as you stand with drug use, is there
drug use going on at this present time?

WH: Who are you talking to?!

WW: To you, Whitney. You.

WH: No! You're not talking to me. I'm a mother. Only my mother has privy to that information. You talk to *your* child about that. Don't ask me no questions like I'm a child. You talk to your baby about her, what she gon' be confronting or what she gotta deal with.

WW: And, ah, and—

WH: Don't ask me like I'm a child, 'cause I'm not a child, Wendy.

WW: My child is a little boy and I will talk to him about drugs—

WH: Well, talk to *him* about that [shit], don't talk to me 'bout that [shit].

WW: But, listen, Whitney—

WH: What, Wendy?!

WW: I will talk to my son about drugs because I have been—

WH: Don't ask me, Wendy! Go on to the next thing.

WW: —where the world speculates where you are—

WH: Trust me, Wendy. Move on!

WW: —which is, uh . . . I was a full-blown cocaine addict, so I—

WH: Well, that's your problem, not mine. Move on.

WW: Well, you—no, that *was* my problem, Whitney.

WH: I'll let you talk to yourself. Did you ask God to help you?

WW: And, no. I, I've managed, thank God. 'Cause I have a good man and—

WH: And so do I!

WW: So, thank God, I was able to just rise up—

WH: Yeah, thank God, Wendy.

WW: —above it and quit and all I asked you, Whitney, is the same thing that many people—

WH: But, Wendy, that's not your business.

WW: Okay, okay. And you on Diane Sawyer also mentioned that, um, you'd want to see receipts behind the drug use.

WH: Shunh, man, if I spent that much money, somebody better gimme some receipts so I can get a tax return.

WW: Well, speaking of spending money . . . So, recently I was hearing that you were trying to trim the budget, which, by the way, Whitney, I thought that this was something—

WH: Well, where the hell you get your information from?! Who's calling you and telling you?

WW: I'm, ah, well I got this story from a gossip, Steve Herrs. Do you know him?

WH: No. Like you said, gossip. Yeah, whatever.

WW: Steve Herrs is a West Coast correspondent and, um, we, I communicate with all the different gossips. It's what we do. You know, uh—

WH: Yeah, so you's all get together and have a gossip lunch, huh?

WW: Something like, something like that. Anyway, Whitney—

WH: Yes.

WW: They're saying that, um, you're doing some massive budget cuts—

WH: I'm doing massive changes.

WW: And, you know what?

WH: Yeah?

WW: I wanted to let you know that this is something I think is good. This is a good thing, Whitney.

WH: You like it, you approve? Yayyy! Wendy approves!

WW: Oh, Whitney, please! Listen, they were saying that you were . . . that you cut your mother's, um—

WH: See, you don't know what the [fuck]—

WW: —allowance.

WH: —you talking about. See, don't make me curse on the radio. I'm trying to be, you know, come on!

WW: Well, Steve was saying it was about like sixteen hundred a week to about five hundred a week. There's—

WH: Tell Steve to kiss my [ass].

WW: Okay. He also—

WH: And so can anybody else who'd ever think I'd do that to my mother. You low-down dirty [bitch].

WW: He also was letting me know that Michael, Gary, and your sister, Donna, who runs your Nippy company, are also, um, experiencing the slashes across the board. They were saying that you have a twenty-four-hour-a-day bar on-site at your studio that you're now cutting down and you're not making your personal chef available to people to just come up in your house and just order food and stuff. I think that's all good.

WH: When did that ever happen? I don't even know what the [hell] you're talking about!

WW: Well—

WH: I have no idea what the [fuck] you're talking about, Wendy.

WW: How is Bobbi Kristina doing?

WH: Glowing. And being a beautiful young lady that God sent her here to be.

WW: Yeah, she's nine now, right?

WH: Yes, she is.

WW: Um, when your husband was, um, incarcerated for those few days. What types of things do you tell her concerning . . . like do you say, Daddy's away visiting Boston?

WH: What are, what are we talking to, a [fucking] retard? She's a, what, a psych patient? She's a child who has intelligence.

WW: Okay.

WH: My child is smart.

WW: No, what I meant—

WH: I talk to her! [Fucking] shush your mouth. I talk to her like she's an intelligent human being. Okay, and I give her just as much as she can handle for a nine year old 'cause I'm her mother, okay. And that's how we deal with it. Never mind what I told her, but she know the deal.

WW: Well, a lot of the, a lot of parents, a lot of parents whose spouse, or what have you, goes through something, particularly because that was only eight days, would have either taken them out of school for the eight days or taken them away from watching TV to, you know, see headlines.

WH: I do what I do to protect my daughter, Wendy—just like you would do to protect your son. Okay? All right?!

WW: You are very defensive, Whitney.

WH: I have to be, Wendy. You talk about me every [fucking] day.

WW: Well—

WH: And every other day.

WW: Whitney, you keep yourself in the headlines.

WH: No, Wendy. Y'all keep me in the headlines. I mind my business. I try to maintain what I got. Y'all wanna know what I'm doing all the time. I don't give a [shit] about what you doing all the time as long as you healthy and God is blessing you and you doing the right thing and being a decent person. I can handle that.

WW: When's the last time you talked to Robin?

WH: About a week ago. Aaahaa!

WW: Because I know that you and Robin were girlfriends from when you were growing up.

WH: And we're still friends, girl!

WW: Okay, will she be working back with you or is she still—

WH: Wendy, Wendy, Wendy, Wendy! What Robin got to do with anything?! No, Robin don't work for me. She don't work for me now. Moving right along. Uh-hunh!

WW: Okay.

WH: Okay, okay!

WW: So, our king of R & B, is he working on an album? Bobby. Is Bobby working on an album?

WH: Yes, ma'am.

WW: When do you think his album will be out?

WH: Uh, very soon, Wendy. I'm sure.

WW: A numerologist came on the show the other day—

WH: (*Yells something and coughs.*)

WW: —and we ran you guys' numbers, and for what it's worth the numerologist said that you and Bobby are so right for each other.

WH: Honey, he's so right. He's never been more right in his life. That's the most rightest thing you've ever said.

WW: Thank you, Whitney.

WH: Unh-hunh!

WW: So, um, have you ever thought of selling your New Jersey estate and relocating to Atlanta?

WH: I relocated to Orlando, but I still own my Jersey estate and I will always keep my Jersey estate.

WW: Mm-hmm.

WH: Unh-hunh.

WW: How is your father doing?

WH: Not well, Wendy. He's very ill.

WW: Yeah. Um, his partner, Kevin Skinner, um . . .

WH: Don't wanna talk about him! Moving right along!

WW: And I didn't talk to him, Whitney.

WH: I don't want to talk about him. He's not my friend, okay?

WW: Okay.

WH: You wanna be my friend? I'd like to be your friend, I think.

WW: Well, you're so defensive. Is this how you treat your friends?

WH: No, but you're not my friend.

WW: You just said you want to be my friend.

WH: I said I *want*. See, see. I want to be your friend.

WW: When's the next—

WH: I'm not saying I *am* your friend.

WW: When's the next time you're going to hit the big screen?

WH: I'm working on it, baby girl. I'm working on it. I got some scripts today. I'm gonna read, read on them and look at them. But, you know, I'm very careful about the movies I do—

WW: Mm-hmm.

WH: So, you know, it's just a matter of time.

WW: Great. So how long do you think that you're going to be, uh, how long will it be between albums? Have you already started mulling over in your head when your next album's going to come out and what kind of material you're going to be working with?

WH: Yes, I am, as a matter of fact.

WW: Have you spoken to Brandy since she had her baby?

WH: Yes, I talked to her. Maybe every week.

WW: Wow!

WH: Yeah.

WW: Because you're, I mean, the kind of money that you have is like, you know, beyond most people's imagination. When dear friends like Brandy have babies, do you actually pick out a gift for them or do you send like an assistant to—

WH: No, no! I pick out my gifts, darling.

WW: Where did you—

WH: People are personal to me; I pick my own gifts out.

WW: What did you get for Brandy?

WH: I got her a, um, silver rattle at, um . . . Tiffany rattle and I got a picture frame that, um, has my name and Bobby's name on it. Auntie Whitney, Uncle Bobby, and Cousin Krissy. And, you know, it's like a family thing so that she has a keepsake for the rest of her life.

WW: That's nice, Whitney.

WH: Yeah.

WW: Do you ever do simple things like go to the grocery store?

WH: Yeah. I was yesterday pumping gas.

WW: Yeah?!

WH: Yeah.

WW: And what kind of car were you putting the gas in?

WH: I was putting gas into a white Hummer.

WW: Wow! And so did you get it in your neighborhood so they're already used to seeing you, or did you get it elsewhere?

WH: No, I got it in my neighborhood.

WW: Do you live a relatively normal life in that area where you live?

WH: No.

WW: You constantly have people in the woods trying to take pictures and all that stuff?

WH: Hello! I mean, come on, Wendy! You don't make it any better. (*Sarcastic chuckle.*) But, um, actually, yeah, I have people in the woods, in the trees, and wanna follow me and, yeah, the whole nine yards, Wendy.

WW: Yeah, yeah. So when it's just you and Bobby, Kristina, in the house, the three of you, who is part of the staff of your house who's always there as well, you know besides—

WH: Jesus. (*Laughs.*)

WW: I got you, I got you.

WH: Jesus. Constantly.

WW: Okay.

WH: Anybody else may come and go, but He's a constant stay.

WW: How's your mom doing? Does she live there in the house—

WH: And she's a constant stay, too, but she does not live with me. No, my mother does not. I have family mostly around me. My brother-in-laws, my sister-in-laws, and my nieces. People like that.

WW: How do you get along with Bobby's babies' mothers?

WH: (*Blows a raspberry.*) You are hysterical, girl. Oh, my God! You are so deep.

WW: I mean—

WH: Oh, you're so like, so, you know, like nosy. Aaaaaah!

WW: I am.

WH: You are so [fucking] nosy, man.

WW: I am. It's not just you. I'm like this with everybody, Whitney.

WH: I know you are. Your son must be like "[Damn], Ma!"

WW: No, he asks the questions that . . . every other word from him is "But why, but why!"

WH: But why! I hear ya, I hear ya. Um, what did you say again?

WW: How do you get along with Bobby's babies' mothers?

WH: We get along just fine. We get along just fine. Because we're grown women and, um, I love her babies because they're my stepchildren and I care for her children, as if you know. They are mine when they're with me. So, um, you maintain that relationship with your stepchildren. Me and Bobby's babies' mamas don't have any problems 'cause I don't create none and if there is some I can finish it. Yeah.

WW: Well.

WH: We can talk about it and get an understanding.

WW: Has there ever been a conflict as far as maybe Bobbi Kristina getting more attention from Bobby—

WH: No.

WW: —than the other kids?

WH: No. There's always that, you know. There's the constant, you know, when the kids get together and they, you know, constant normal [shit], but you know, basically, um, you know, it's pretty normal. But Bobby gives his children, you know, this kind of attention that when they're together, they're his children.

WW: Yeah.

WH: But of course, you know, he's my husband and he lives with me and Krissy, so she does get more of his time.

WW: Did you get on Bobby after you saw the BET "Making of Ja Rule's Video?" 'Cause the rest of the country was kind of like "Wow, look at Bobby!" Bobby looked kind of tossed up during that video, Whitney.

WH: Did he really, now?

WW: Bobby looked high, Whitney.

WH: He did?

WW: Bobby looked [fuuuucked] up.

WH: (*Hysterical laughter.*)

WW: (*Laughs.*)

WH: But, see, there was Ja Rule in there, there was Bobby, there were other folk, but you ain't say [shit] about them.

WW: Yeah, but, but . . . Bobby—

WH: Yeah, yeah, yeah, 'cause all you wanted to concentrate on is Bobby. No, as a matter of fact, Bobby was pretty cool, honey. He did his gig. He's Thug Lovin'. What?! Fine, shoop, shoop, talk to me, unh-huh. That's what I heard.

WW: Is, is, is Bobby . . . I realize that being married, you know, your money is you know, Bobby's money and vice versa—

WH: Right.

WW: —but, um, when, you know, so you guys don't have any money problems—

WH: Well, no, Wendy, not to sell my estate as you said on the radio yesterday.

WW: Oh, no, I didn't say you were selling your estate for money reasons. I said you were selling your estate to get more privacy, you know—

WH: Oh, I understand. No, no, okay, thank you, darling, for clarifying that. No, I'm not selling my estate and Bobby and I are doing just fine, thank you.

WW: Were you responsible for Bobby leaving New Edition?

WH: I didn't even know him then.

WW: No, no, no, no—the second time around, when they did the "Come Home" tour?

WH: No. No. I say not at all. They had their own relationship.

WW: Have you ever encouraged Bobby to, uh, possibly, you know . . . Because the guys from New Edition, um, have interviewed and said that they would love it if Bobby came back, you know, to—

WH: That's Bobby's world; it's not mine. It's his decision. He's a New Edition member, I'm not.

WW: Did you ever hear that people were buzzing that your relationship with Wyclef was really close and that Bobby and you fought over it?

WH: You? Really?

WW: Yeah.

WH: No, no, no, we don't do that! Wyclef and I are friends. We grew up together in the hood. He's from East Orange and so am I. And, um, that's about as far as that goes. And we musically work together. That's it. There is no battle, there's no fighting. That's crazy.

WW: Well, at one point there was a beef between Bobby and Babyface.

WH: Oh, really?

WW: Yeah.

WH: Well, why don't you talk to Bobby and Babyface about that?

WW: You know what, Whitney?

WH: What, baby?

WW: You are something else! (*Laughs.*)

WH: I've been waiting to talk to you. I love you, darling.

WW: When are you coming to the studio?

WH: When am I coming to *your* studio?

WW: Yeah.

WH: You really want me to come there?

WW: I would love that.

WH: Oh, my lord. Well, we gonna make a date, okay?

WW: Yes, we will. Look, do you want to have more children?

WH: Yes, I do. I want a little boy.

WW: Hmm.

WH: I want a mama's boy.

WW: And you're going to be forty this year, right?

WH: Oh, tell the world, why don't ya! Oh, you low-down dirty dog!

WW: Whitney, you look great.

WH: Woo, thank you, baby. I feel good, too, thank you.

WW: I mean, the only thing is that you said, um, "Whitney will never be fat!"

WH: No.

WW: I was like "How dare her!"

WH: Never.

WW: What was that?! A dis to all fat girls?

WH: No. I just won't be fat. Sorry, not good, not healthy. Have you ever heard of anyone being fat being healthy?

WW: Well, you know, being extremely fat or being extremely thin like you on the Michael Jackson special . . .

WH: Well, either extreme is not good.

WW: Yeah.

WH: Not good at all, okay?

WW: Yeah.

WH: Not good at all. So, uh, pull it together and move on.

WW: You smoke weed?

WH: Oh, [shit]! (*Laughs.*)

WW: (*Laughs.*) Mariah Carey was on the show and said that she loves you more than ever.

WH: I love that little lamb chop.

WW: And I just wanted to let you know that. How do you feel—

WH: I love that lamb chop; she's my girl.

WW: Have you uh . . . yeah, she is nice; she's very sweet. She was here like two weeks ago.

WH: Yeah. She's the bomb.

WW: She denied her breast implants. Do you deny yours?

WH: Ah, [fuck] no!

WW: See, that's my girl, Whitney.

WH: No. No.

WW: I got 'em too. I mean, aren't they the best?

WH: No, I mean, you know, it's like what. I mean, you know, if you're gonna go for it, go for it, you know what I mean?

WW: Do you ever wish that you got 'em bigger?

WH: No, my husband loves them.

WW: Yeah, yeah, yeah, yeah, yeah!

WH: He looooves them!

WW: Yeah. They sit nice. They're very well proportioned with you. It's just that at one point when you lost so much weight, though, they did look like two baseballs on a stick.

WH: Yeah. They looked really weird.

WW: (Laughs.)

WH: Absolutely. I'm sure that when you look at yourself in the mirror you have some reservations about your looks too.

WW: Absolutely.

WH: (Teasing laughter.)

WW: (Club Cheetah "yayayaya" yell.)

WH: Child, please!

WW: Absolu—

WH: I seen you, I know how you look. (Laughs.)

WW: Uhhh, what? (Laughs.)

WH: Come on, Wendy, more. Come on, baby.

WW: Do you keep in touch with Eddie Murphy? I know you guys were uh—

WH: No.

WW: Now, is it that you are showing respect for your husband because you and Eddie dated or—

WH: Yeah.

WW: Got you. Well that's, to me, that's how it's supposed to be in everyday life. You know what I'm saying? When you go on and you marry somebody—

WH: Come on, Wendy, he's a married man and I'm a married woman. I mean, we see each other, we speak to each other professionally and say good-bye, that's it.

WW: Yeah, yeah.

WH: Yeah.

WW: Bobby, um, has had a reputation occasionally to step out on the marriage.

WH: Oh, really?

WW: Say the gossips.

WH: Okay, thank you.

WW: Has infidelity been one of the biggest issues in you guys' marriage?

WH: No.

WW: What would you say the biggest issue is in you all's marriage?

WH: You people. You [fucking] people who like to run your [damn] mouths. Unh-huh. Yeah!

WW: Hmm?

WH: Unh.

WW: If you could take back anything that you told Diane Sawyer, what would it be?

WH: (*Sucks her teeth.*) If I could, if I could say something that I didn't say, okay, I want to tell anybody that got a problem with Whitney to kiss my [ass]. And I love you, but I don't live for you. I don't live for you. You talk about me, you call me out my name, you, you make my mother call me and ask me questions, you make my father sick, you make my brother sick, you make my child hurt. You all talk about me like you know me. You ain't never met me, ain't never seen me in your damn life, but you talk about me. That's not right. There's a limit to what you can say. And if I was really like back in the day in Newark, I'd meet you outside. I'd meet you outside, but I'm a lady and I have class. But I'll talk to you, Wendy, 'cause I love you 'cause you a fan, I know it.

WW: I am.

WH: I know it, baby.

WW: I'm a fan of your entire experience, not just—

WH: 'Cause I'm from Newark. I'll tell you something, I don't take no [shit] like that. Those are fighting words sometimes you say.

WW: (Sighs.) You know what, though?

WH: What, boo?

WW: I'm a fan of yours. Not just the music, Whitney. I'm a fan of you, the woman.

WH: Thank you. 'Cause my mother is very proud of me, Wendy. She is, she loves me and she respects me. That's what matters to me. That my mother loves and respects me.

WW: Whose idea was it to set up that Diane Sawyer interview?

WH: Me and L.A. [Reid, head of Arista].

WW: Are you done with the talk show circuit? I mean, will you do Larry King?

WH: Yeeep, done!

WW: So you won't go back on Oprah, you won't do Larry King?

WH: Oprah and I have a relationship. She and I talk. We'll do something. That's my girl. Yeah.

WW: Do any of your, um, celebrity girlfriends, whether it be Oprah or Angela Bassett or anybody like that—do they

	ever try to like, um, ride the train of is Whitney on coke and let me talk to her to get her off?
WH:	(*Inhales.*) You know, they make you to break you. You know what I mean? That's the name of the game. But I don't break. I'm not made out of glass, baby. I come from a line of heritage of strong heritage, legacy. You can't break me.
WW:	So when you sit down and have a little glass of something to drink, what's your favorite drink?
WH:	(*Inhales.*)
WW:	I mean, you know, is it Cristal? Is it, you know, Hennessy?
WH:	Nah, I'm not a drinker, baby. I like to have a sip of wine every now and then and a little, um, there's a drink me and Bobby have called the Bobby Brown. I'm not gonna tell you what it's mixed with, all right?
WW:	God, Whitney!
WH:	What, baby?
WW:	You are a real trip.
WH:	I been around the world.
WW:	Yeahhhh!
WH:	(*Chuckles.*) Yeahhhh!
WW:	How's Dionne doing?
WH:	Dionne's doing very well, thank you. We got an auntie who just passed away. A very close auntie to my heart and we just buried her last week and I saw Dionne and it was really good to see my lady.
WW:	Yeah?
WH:	Yeah.
WW:	So, your father's hundred-million-dollar lawsuit, is that done?
WH:	[Bullshit.]
WW:	It's, okay. And you guys are . . . He's dropped the lawsuit and it's—
WH:	It's [bullshit], Wendy. I love my daddy, my daddy loves me.
WW:	I believe that, Whitney.

WH: No, know it.

WW: I thought it was some mess when I saw it going down. I—

WH: [Bullshit]

WW: Um. Do you think that, um, although your parents are divorced, them worrying about you in this demonic thing called show business—

WH: Unh-hunh.

WW: —you think that keeps them together in their own way?

WH: Yes.

WW: Hmm. Your father, um, wasn't your father dating or married or something like that to a—

WH: He's married now.

WW: That's right

WH: To another wife.

WW: How do you get along with your stepmom?

WH: Just fine. I get along with Peggy just fine.

WW: Peggy.

WH: We get along just fine. She's a sweet lady.

WW: Does your mom date?

WH: Yes, she does. She minds her business too.

WW: So, how will you be spending Valentine's Day?

WH: With my husband.

WW: I bet you all have wild, circus sex, don't you?

WH: (*Inhales.*) Oh, my God! Wendy, don't make me meet you outside. Come on, now, you getting too deep.

WW: But I can just pic— It, you . . .

WH: You can picture it, couldn't you?

WW: Yeah!

WH: Ya nasty-ass bitch!

WW: You are such passionate people.

WH: You're nasty, boo. (*Snickers.*)

WW: Just wild, circus sex!

WH: (*Laughs.*)

WW: You know what, Whitney? Would you . . .

WH: What?

WW: Would you ever think about writing a book on your life?

WH: I might, somewhere down the line.

WW: I wrote a book. It's with Atria Books.

WH: Mm-hmm.

WW: They're a boutique label of Simon and Schuster and it comes out in the fall of 2003.

WH: Oh, I'mma get it!

WW: And I just found that—

WH: Are you writing it yourself?

WW: Yes, I am.

WH: Good.

WW: Yeah, you want to know what, Whitney?

WH: What, baby?

WW: I found that it was the most therapeutic thing—

WH: I know. I know.

WW: —that I've ever done in my life.

WH: I know. See, I do that but I do it with my spiritual partner. You know what I'm saying? You know. I do it with my prayer partner and that's my therapy.

WW: Do you still go to church?

WH: Yeah.

WW: What church do you go to?

WH: Umm, when I feel like it, it's right there in my heart.

WW: Okay, okay, I got you.

WH: Mm-hmm.

WW: Well, Whitney. I want to thank you—

WH: Thank you, Wendy!

WW: —for giving me this moment and not hanging up the phone.

WH: No, I wouldn't do that to you, baby. I'mma talk through.

WW: And being as sassy as you want to be.

WH: (*Laughs.*) Wendy, I love you! 'Cause you support me and you been good to me on the radio. However, watch what you say, baby girl.

WW: But, Whitney, watch what you do. And if it—

WH: I know it's not—You don't even know what I do. Like you said, you never met me, you don't know me, you ain't been in my house, you don't live with me, you don't sleep with me, you don't do [shit] for me but talk about me. So watch what you say. That's all, baby girl. That's all I'm asking you, is watch what the [fuck] you say.

WW: But, Whitney—

WH: What, baby?

WW: —I would love to have you come in the studio.

WH: Okay, love. We'll make a date. You call my machine, I'll call yours.

WW: I would love to be able to—

WH: All right

WW: —read your body language as—

WH: Ooh, you don't have any idea. I'm sitting here chilling on the Miami balcony just talking to you.

WW: Are you?

WH: Yeah, baby. Just finished eating some chicken.

WW: What's the weather like?

WH: It's like seventy-four [degrees].

WW: And who all's in the room there?

WH: Yeah, just my dog and my secretary and Joey from A, from Arista Records, who is pacing the floor.

WW: And—Now, why is Joey pacing? He wants you to hang—

WH: 'Cause he's like, you know, you, you don't . . . you feeling froggy, you better not leap. (*Giggles.*)

232

WW: Umm, Whitney, have you ever, has it ever gotten so bad where you ever would consider suicide?

WH: Hell, no! I got a child to live for. Come on.

WW: That's what I'm talking about.

WH: Work with me. I won't leave you.

WW: I love you, Whitney.

WH: I love you, too, Wendy.

WW: You take care.

WH: You, too, baby.

WW: Bye.

WH: Be blessed.

CHAPTER
14

Advice Hour

I started giving advice in 1999 when I was in Philadelphia—after being run out of New York. A lot had changed in my life, and I woke up one day and realized, "Damn! I have been through a lot!" And perhaps I had something to offer my listeners beyond the who-is-doing-who gossip items or what all was going on in the world of celebrities.

I was drug free—finally! After being strung out on cocaine for more than ten years, I finally had a clear mind. Philadelphia also gave me time to breathe. It wasn't New York City, which in many ways made me extremely callous dealing with not only the culture but also the nastiness of the "business." I got to see life in its purest form.

I got married while I was in Philly. I had two tragic miscarriages and finally delivered my baby boy while in Philly. I had major plastic surgery while there. I would be talking to listeners and all of a sudden, I would find them asking me questions about the things I was talking about on the air—my life.

I gained more than a hundred pounds when I was pregnant. I'd had liposuction on my thighs and stomach several years before this and when I gained all of that weight, the fat came back in the strangest places. Thank God, it didn't settle on my neck or in my face, as many people have complained has happened to them. But it came back on my inner thighs and my back. I had the fattest back in the universe. And I talked about it on the air (Note: generally when you get liposuction and you gain weight, it doesn't return to those places where the fat was sucked.)

I went back and got liposuction on my inner thighs and back and had a tummy tuck after I gave birth to my son. And people started calling in and asking me questions about plastic surgery.

I used my show as a platform to vent about things that were happening to me, and I realized that I was not alone. Those years I spent in a cocaine stupor, I didn't really care about what was going on around me, and I was so paranoid that I wasn't sharing anything that I was doing. But with a clear head, I found out that I wasn't so alone in the things that I was thinking and doing in my life. And I also found out that if people were calling *me* for advice, they were just as clueless as I was. Hell, I was trying to navigate through life too. We might as well get through it together.

So advice hour was born.

I will say this right up front—I don't have any expertise or any clinical background to give advice. The advice I give is simply my opinion or my take on a particular situation, so don't sue me if you take my advice and things get screwed up. That's on you. And don't get mad if you ask for my advice and don't like the answer that I give. If you're asking me, you obviously haven't figured it out for yourself and I'm just giving you my honest opinion on your situation. So if you don't want the truth, don't ask me.

It really amazed me that when I took time through sobriety to really listen to people and hear their problems, they needed help with the simplest things. I would get a lot of "I wear a size eleven shoe and I hear you talking about your feet being big. Where do you buy your shoes?" People were looking at me as the Pied Piper of the big foot. I would even get people asking my advice on finding a good ob-gyn—like I was the Yellow Pages or something.

But most of the advice people requested was relationship advice: "I caught my man cheating, what should I do?" or "I have three kids by three different men and I want my current boyfriend to marry me," or "I am a single man and I want to meet a nice woman."

There was very little that I couldn't relate to. I was no longer a twenty-something cocaine addict too selfish in my shit to think clearly. I was a married woman who had been struggling to have a baby and finally did. I came from a suburban, two-parent background and was college educated and married to a man who was a thug. I had been divorced and cheated on. I could talk about everything from drug addiction and liposuction to fake hair.

I'm proud of the things that I've done and the things that I have overcome. I'm proud of the things that I'm scared of and the things that I've conquered. And I have no shame. I feel that is one of the advantages I have over people like Oprah and Star Jones— there is nothing that I will not talk about, because I have no shame about anything that I have done.

I have been through enough in my life to share with you all the things that I have learned. I have made enough mistakes and had enough disappointment to be able to relate to most situations.

You never know how much of an impact you can have on people. You never know how much the things you share or your perspective on life can change people. I was stopped by a woman on the street who is five feet eleven like me. She stopped me to thank me because she said I had given her the courage to stand tall. I often talk about my height and how important it is for tall women to stand tall and straight and not slouch. And she took my advice.

Looking at this woman, I would never have suspected that she wouldn't walk tall or that she would have any insecurities. She was one of those beautiful women who seem to exude confidence. She had a great body, great skin, great hair. Just a natural beauty. And she came over and thanked *me*? I am happy that I was able to make her feel good about herself.

With women it's so hard sometimes. We can be so catty. So bitchy. We seem to have a hard time supporting one another. I admit, I came up in the industry believing that every other woman was my enemy. But I learned that couldn't be further from the truth.

I was on my way to being a catty bitch, but that was nipped in the bud by women who paved the way for me. The women ahead of me in the business showed me that there is enough for all of us. And I never got a chance to execute my cattiness. Carol Ford, Yvonne Mobley, Kathy Hughes, all gave me a solid foundation on how to be a woman in this business and how to pave the way for others. I can honestly say as far as being a mentor I have had problems with only one woman in this game. And that was because she fell into that catty BS.

To get this far and actually have someone jump up like they're going to take it all from you, like I didn't pay my dues, that it's just that easy, like I'm going to let a bitch jump up and be a bad bitch, well, that simply wasn't going to happen. Needless to say, she is now off my radar at this point.

And I've only had one other particularly catty experience with someone I didn't expect to see that from. Mo'Nique, who hosts *It's Showtime at the Apollo,* and who starred on the since-cancelled *The Parkers,* was brand-new in the industry when we met in the early 1990s.

We weren't close friends, but we were being teamed up for a pilot for a new television talk show. We had a deal with Buena Vista Disney and we were going to be the next big thing. They discovered Mo'Nique through the comedy circuit and I was one of the most popular deejays in New York. We flew out to Los Angeles and shot several pilots for this show.

We shot some pilots in New York as well. And we were hanging together for a minute. She was even there the night my husband proposed to me at the club. In fact, she got dressed at my house that night. I remember helping her zip her dress.

We had a lot in common, both being big girls, both trying to break into television. But we were also very different. While Mo'Nique was content to make her name being a big girl, I didn't want to be known for being big. I wasn't happy with my body and I think that my desire to get breast implants and liposuction somehow insulted Mo'Nique.

We never got the television show. And we went our separate ways. And when she started blowing up on *The Parkers* she became a subject for the wags, the gossips. She had made her way into Cindy Adams's, and Liz Smith's columns. And once she made it to that level she was more than subject to being talked about on my show. I was simply reading from the gossip pages about her messy marriage and divorce. She took offense to me talking about it. But it was somehow okay for the others to talk about her.

It was difficult for Mo'Nique to reckon with that fact that I am a force in the industry, and even though I knew her before, she is a star and she's on my radar. If you're going through relationship problems, I'm going to talk about you. I believe she expected me to do her a solid and not do my job. She didn't really expect that I would talk about her. And that's good. This is what I do, however.

I don't have any problems with Mo'Nique. I wish her well. But I don't think that sentiment goes both ways. When she was doing her stand-up in New York City, she managed to work me into her act, calling me a drag queen. I guess she needed regional material, the material used for a specific area outside of the usual jokes that will bring New Yorkers into her fold. So she would start off with "Wendy is a drag queen." She would just throw me into her bit. I'm very flattered to be a part of her stand-up routine. I understand the rules. I didn't make them, but I certainly do understand them.

But it is a bit sad. What's also sad are not only the things women do to one another but the things women do to themselves over men.

I interviewed Jennifer Lopez when she was engaged to Ben Affleck, and I felt that it wasn't a match made in heaven. I felt a sadness when she talked about the relationship and she started getting misty. Now, here is a woman with absolutely everything— a great movie career, a successful recording career. She is known as one of the most beautiful people in Hollywood. She has money, fame, and success. But she just can't get it right when it comes to relationships.

There are women who enjoy being in relationships who can do it with a degree of a sanity, and then there are women who insanely go from relationship to relationship. Jennifer Lopez and Elizabeth Taylor are insane with their man-hopping. Paris Hilton man-hops too—without, however, getting into a relationship—bordering on marriage—with everyone she is rumored to be involved with. But who knows if one is better than the other?

I look at J.Lo with a certain amount of sadness. Apparently, she would do very, very well just being by herself for a moment and getting into herself and enjoying her own fame, success, and womanhood and all of that other stuff—that good stuff that women push to the side when they are with a man. But I know by the time this book comes out, she will probably be engaged to someone else or married.

There are women like J.Lo, then there are women like Star Jones. I don't believe J.Lo really knows what she wants. I believe Star Jones knows exactly what she wants and she is willing to do what she has to do to get it.

The View's Star Jones got engaged on national television during halftime at the 2004 All-Star game in Los Angeles. She's been a basketball fan for a long time, so it was no shock for her to be at All-Star Weekend with great seats, watching the event. She has recently lost a great deal of weight through what I understand was stomach stapling. I applaud her effort to lose weight, and she's starting to look really great. Star was definitely morbidly obese and clearly an attractive woman with great potential to be a world-class beauty. And she's very smart.

She had been seeing Al Reynolds for four or five months. They met at an Alicia Keys album release party in New York in 2003. It was a celebrity event—not open to the public, by invitation only. Yes, I was invited. No, I didn't go. That is my usual MO when it comes to events like this. I am invited just as much as I'm not invited. My position remains the same—I'm busy. It could be as simple as I want to get home and see my kid.

So I didn't go to this event. Star was there—as well she should have been. She's a single woman with a great job in the city, no kids, able to go and live the life. The way she told it on *The View*, she was navigating her way through the crowd with her glass of champagne and she passed this man and he said, "I know you're not going to pass me like that." And someone standing near them introduced Al to Star. While Alicia was performing, he supposedly came up behind her and swayed with her to the music.

Single woman meets single man at a fabulous party in New York City and bombs burst, rockets fly, and four months later, they're engaged. There is a beautiful five-carat princess ring. Beyoncé and Jay-Z, Denzel and Paulette, Jimmy Jam and his wife, are all courtside to witness. It was great for Star. Was this desperation, as many have said since?

When you're forty-one years old and you meet someone that you like, to get engaged that quickly is not surprising. At that age you know what you do or don't want out of life. You know where you want to navigate your career. You know when your retirement kicks in and where you're headed with your finances. And you know what you don't want out of your companion. You know what you're willing to put up with—whether he be a philandering man, a gay man, an unemployed man, a man who makes less money than you. And you know whether you want children.

When I heard Star and Al got engaged, I was not surprised at all. She talks cocky, she and her all-girl crew. But you hear the wanting in her voice. It sounds very modern and very *Sex and the City*-ish. I don't know whether it's the more successful you get or the older you get, but companionship for women is important. It's very important.

Now, I have received a lot of behind-the-scenes gossip about Star's fiancé. Since his picture has been splashed on all of the gossip pages I have gotten a lot of "Wendy, guess what . . . ?" The

Daily News even reported that Al Reynolds at one point "played for the other team," meaning he had relations with men. I am not going to explore any of that. As he said through his publicist in the article, "that's between me and my fiancée."

That is between Star and her man. I wish Star Jones happiness, because she appears to have it all. And to have a partner with whom to share all that she has is very important. It's very important. Watching *Sex and the City* makes it seem too easy to be single and carefree. But most women—even the most powerful, successful, wealthiest women—want someone to share it with. I don't care what they say. And if Star has found her man, I pump my fist for her. And her fiancé, Al Reynolds, is getting a complete package of a complete woman. He's meeting her at a good time. He's meeting her as a fatso but will end up with a woman with nice proportions, who has loads of money, and an education, and whose forty-plus years of sassiness and courage, as well as genuine fears and vulnerability, make her a real woman. I wish them luck. I give it three years.

CHAPTER
15
Ask Wendy

WENDY:

I am a single black woman in my mid thirties who has never been married and would like to be. I cannot seem to meet the right man. I have gone to church, the mall, even the supermarket, and have not found a man who I feel I connect with. What am I doing wrong?

—LILY

LILY:

If I were you, I would take my search to the Internet—yes, the Internet. There are so many dating sites online now and to tell you the truth, many people report back to me that they have found some success dating online.

I do have a few cautionary words: Be honest, because he probably will not be honest, and that will give you the upper hand. Men mostly lie about their height and looks and finances; you must tell the truth. I also suggest that your first few dates be in a very public place. I mean, let's be honest, there are a few nuts out there, and you don't want to be stuck someplace where you can't make a quick exit if you get one of those nuts.

I happen to love coffee shops, and I suggest you meet during the day—either for breakfast or lunch. Don't let the date last longer than two hours, and the date should start and end at that coffee shop. Don't make plans to meet later—even if you hit it off. Wait. I would suggest that the coffee-shop meeting spot should last for at least four dates, until you really get to know this guy.

Don't give too many details about your personal life either. If you're a securities trader, don't let him know exactly where you work on Wall Street. If you live in Queens, don't let him know exactly what block. And hopefully the coffee shop won't be right at the curb, it will be in the mall, where your car can be mixed up among all the other cars. Don't let him see your license plate, because he can get a lot of information about you from your plates. Caution. Caution. Caution.

With those precautions, I definitely recommend Internet dating. I also like personal ads. I love personal ads and have actually had a couple of dates from the personal ads myself. But you must apply the same rules as with Internet dating. Caution. Caution. Caution.

I also suggest dating across racial lines. That's big for some people. Yes, I have to be perfectly honest with you, I never thought about marrying a white man. I didn't feel the need to look across racial lines. I don't have a "down on black man" thing in my life because I have a father, uncles, and a brother who have all given me very positive images of black men and I never had a reason to look at a white man, a Puerto Rican man, or any other man other than a black man for comfort.

But I will tell you, if I was out there today, I might consider it. I have dated outside my race and if I were a single girl looking at the slim pickings, I would have to look elsewhere for a mate. My best girlfriend from high school is married to a white man and they are a great couple. I just find that black works for me. But if you're single and you're thirty-three, thirty-seven, forty, honey, you need to do something if you want to get married! And if you don't want to get married, then fall back.

And I have a question for you, Lily. How do you leave the house? Do you leave the house looking like a woman who is available? By that I mean, do you make sure you throw on some lipstick and your hair is halfway decent?

You never know who you may encounter while running to the post office or dropping into the local drugstore. I'm not suggesting you have to get your hair done or have on full-blown makeup for everyday things, I'm just saying that even on the weekend you should look cute—cute enough to not be embarrassed if you see a man who catches your eye. Even if you're bummy, you should be cute bummy. Because you are single and you are looking.

Lily, I also suggest hitting nightclubs—which many people say are horrible places to meet men. I disagree. There are many nightspots that host after-work events that are wonderful places to meet men. I like the watering holes, myself—the ones that get a decent crowd in the place by nine o'clock at night. Because ain't nothing but the devil is out after midnight. I believe that.

DEAR WENDY,

I am with a man who came to me with lots of baggage. And two years later we're still going strong. Baggage doesn't necessarily mean that people can't be good in relationships, but the woman has to be ready to deal with everything that comes with it.

I'm a young, very attractive attorney. When me and my man got together, I knew him for a couple of months and he soon became homeless. He had a young daughter who he has full custody of and had no job when I got with him, but I saw past all of that because I knew he was a good man. He wasn't a thug or anything like that. I helped him get back on his feet, got us an apartment, and helped him with his daughter. I got him the paper and helped him with some job leads.

Now we are engaged and he's making good money as a programmer. He is no longer dependent on me and he spends his extra cash on me.

I would like you to share this with the ladies in your audience to encourage them that there are some nuggets of gold buried in the dirt.

—SHEILA

SHEILA,

Hmm. I am not sure if I agree with you. I think you were just lucky.

That said, you are right, there are some good men out there who may have fallen on bad times. But I will say this—it couldn't be me. (Also, by the way, a thug is not necessarily a bad guy, as you suggest.)

What you did, I couldn't do. I do not have the patience. God bless you. You never know what you're going to dust off and what kind of gold you have if you just stick it out. But it couldn't be me.

Your man was homeless *with* a young daughter. And as you said, "I got *us* an apartment," and you got him a paper and had to push him in the right direction and call on contacts and all of that. Hell, no! Hell, no!

But . . . you never know. Sometimes you have got to pick the wild card, because you never know how it's going to end up. See, you got a great one. But I still think you just lucked out.

DEAR WENDY,

I've been with my baby's father for about three years and we argue almost every day. And when we do, most of the time it gets physical. Sometimes I'm scared of him. Sometimes he makes me want to leave him, but I'm scared that he will do something to me. There is someone at work who calls me and makes me happy. He tells me things I want to hear. My baby's father calls me everything in the book—dumb, bitch, and ugly. What do I do? I'm eighteen; my baby's father is twenty-one.

—NO NAME

WENDY'S ADVICE:

Well, you see, the big part of the problem with this letter is that the young lady had her baby too young. The other part of the problem is that she's taken no time out for herself because she can't—she's got a baby, she's eighteen, she's got to grind. She doesn't say what kind of job she has but I can bet that it's a job, not a career. She's scared to leave because she's built no foundation of strength for herself.

Women—and this is my advice to all women of all ages—must build a foundation for themselves.

Women should always stash money away for themselves when they are in a relationship—I don't care whether you're married, whether you're living together, whether you're simply dating. No matter the situation, every mother is doing her daughter a disservice if she doesn't at least tell her that and teach by example about stashing money. And if your mother didn't tell you, I am. Take heed.

That's your money for a rainy day. That's money if he just ups and leaves you. That's money for you if you lose your job. You never know what that stash is going to be for. It could even be money for your family if your man loses his job and now you need to go to your stash to help your family out.

Okay, how do you build a stash? You go to the bank, open up an account in your name only (an account only you know about), and you proceed to put money in there. The money should be the money you put in after your bills are paid with the household and after your kids are taken care of. That little money you would use for the new pair of Jimmy Choo shoes or tax-free shopping day over at H & M, where you might blow three hundred to five hundred dollars, put that money away for you. That's your "fuck-you!" fund. I'm big on fuck-you money. It's the first step to building your foundation. And I suggest you start doing this as early as possible. And it's never too late to start building a foundation.

A woman with a foundation is never scared to leave. She might be a little nervous, but she executes and she does it because that's what she has to do. Some women get the idea that they *have* to be with a man—as in the case of this eighteen-year-old, who is talking about some man at work who is saying the "right things" and making her feel good. Pu-lease! The thing that is luring her from her relationship is the man at her job telling her what she wants to hear—not the man whipping her ass at home. That man at her job doesn't really want her! No disrespect, but nobody wants an eighteen-year-old girl with a baby and a crazy baby's daddy. Right?

This girl's got nothing to offer anybody. This girl's so worried about the men that she can't even concentrate on her own well-being. And her own well-being is the key to being a good mother to her child. She needs to leave all of the men alone.

And this physical abuse happens all too often with these young girls, because men prey on them. And the girls get it in their heads that they *are* fat and dumb and ugly. Older men love this. But if she has a foundation, he can't step to her and exploit that.

By the way, a foundation is more than money, it is also about self-esteem, the way you feel about yourself.

My advice to this poor girl is to go home to your mother, and tell your mother this story. If your mother isn't around, tell your grandmother or an aunt or a godmother—tell some wise woman in your life who cares about you. Tell her the very same story you told me and see what she says. Do not go to your eighteen-year-old girlfriend, because she has little to offer in the way of advice. That's the blind leading the blind. And if she's not chasing men and having babies like you, then she really has nothing in common with you to share and probably does not want to be bothered with your mess.

Talk to a wise family member and purge and get some help for yourself. And more importantly, leave these men alone. Concentrate on building yourself up. There is a reason why the flight attendant on an airplane instructs you in case of an emergency to put the oxygen mask on *your* face first and then place the mask on your child. They don't tell you to mask the child, then mask yourself, because a child needs its mother and a child needs its mother sane and whole and prepared.

It's not too late for this young girl, but she's got to get it together now.

Don't let any man hit you and if you're one of those provoking girls, you need to stop! A lot of women say the worst stuff to their men and wonder why when he hauls off and hits them. You cannot beat a man down with words and turn around and be shocked that he has smacked the hell out of you.

It's tough enough being a black man these days. And shout out to all the black men! This is not me sticking up for you all, but in this particular case I am. Being married to a black man I see how tough it is out here in society. If you work on Wall Street you are still a nigga. If you sell dope on the corner you're still a nigga. Society doesn't know how to separate you all. You get stopped while you're driving for being black. You get looked at as criminals as white women clutch their purses when you walk by. It's tough. I'm not saying that you all need to be handled with kid gloves, but a little extra care and a little extra sensitivity is in order.

That's why in my opinion nobody handles a black man like a black woman. But that's another book for another time.

WENDY:

I need some advice. I'm a thirty-two-year-old white Latina, very independent and self-sufficient. And I have two kids. I've been talking to/seeing a premier NFL football player where I live. Over the past two years we have crossed paths at the grocery store and in the neighborhood. We started talking in September and spent two months talking before going out on our first date. Since our first date we have talked every day and seen each other a couple of times a week. We have been going to the movies, to dinner, he comes to my house, I go to his house.

His team has since lost the play-offs and now it is off-season. He has multiple houses in different parts of the United States and only occasionally comes back where we live during the off-season. I think we've built a legitimate friendship and there is a definite interest on both of our parts, but there hasn't been enough time spent to establish anything solid.

As of late, though, I have been showing more interest in the situation than he seems to be. And he seems to be backing off a little. I'm not good at the whole dating process and I don't want to mess things up at this point, but I already may have. I think his initial attraction to me was that I didn't pay too much attention to him. But things have progressed and I'm not that hard-to-get person anymore.

My question is, since over the past couple of weeks I have been more available and I jumped when he's called, is it too late to back up and gain his interest to where it was?

—JASMINE

PS: My sons' father is an athlete, but we fell in love after three weeks and were together eight years. So even though I've seen the game with athletes and I know all about the groupies with the jump-off situation and how it goes down, I do think there was more, but I don't want to be naïve. Any advice is welcome. Thanks.

JASMINE:

I don't think that it's too late for you to back off and play that hard-to-get role again. I don't think it's too late. But you must be realistic: You are thirty-two with two kids. And unfortunately, the chances of an NFL player really digging the scene—and I'm talking about love, marriage, and the baby carriage—with a thirty-two-year-old woman with two kids are slim to none. I'll be honest—and, remember, I'm not professional, I just an-swer these questions based on my particular experience and my observation—an NFL football player, if he has his pick of all kinds of women all over the place, is going to go for the twenty-five-year-old with no children, with a more flexible schedule who is able to travel with him. Because if it is love and marriage and baby carriage, she can just pick up and go. You've got two kids and you're thirty-two.

You can back up and play aloof and play hard-to-get and see what happens. I don't think it looks good. I think he has put the writing on the wall, and you just don't seem to see it. You're his in-town jump-off. But you never know.

I know the draw of athletes, rappers, and movie stars, but they are such dogs. And it's bad enough that men are doggish to begin with, that we all have to worry about our men cheating and we all have to worry about the lure of other women. But a star athlete, rapper, or actor? I couldn't deal with it at all. That's an interesting world to dabble in, and when you're eighty years old you'll have great stories to tell, but the heartache that accompanies situations like this is crazy.

I get a few letters from women who are dealing with or have dealt with athletes or rappers and actors. And they all have the same story. I mean, by the time somebody is asking me for advice they really don't have anyone else to ask. You know how pissed off the rappers get when they find out that their baby's mother is talking to me? What?! Do you know how bad it must be for a rapper's baby's mother to even come and want to talk to me as opposed to one of her girlfriends?

But you see, once they hook up with one of those stars, either their girlfriend is sleeping with him, too, or their girlfriend is hating on them hard. So at the end of the day, they really have no one to talk to. So they talk to me. And by then they are in too deep—they are a couple of kids in deep when they discover he's secretly married or has given them herpes or also likes to sleep with men. It's crazy.

I got a letter from a girl one day, a twenty-year-old, who was telling me she spent one week in a luxurious Manhattan hotel room with a rapper. She tried coke for the first time, she tried E (Ecstasy) for the first time. And during this glorious week, this rapper gave her herpes.

This letter was a real heartbreaker for me, because I had been hearing whispers about this same rapper that was becoming loud talk that he was infected with HIV. So if this young lady got herpes from unprotected sex, what else had he given her that she may not find out about for a while?

This rapper has been looking sick. The last time I saw him he didn't look well—he had lost a lot of weight and his skin was sallow. But he was blaming it on other issues.

This particular rapper's modus operandi is well known—he loves young girls around seventeen and eighteen years old. He gets them high on E pills, weed, coke, and champagne. And by the time he gets their clothes off he knows no one is looking for sores or asking questions.

This girl writing me about herpes with this same rapper, what am I supposed to do with the other info that I have that he has HIV?

It's terrible watching him rap himself into a grave while slaying young girls all the way. To kill himself is one thing, but to take others with him is criminal. And he targets young girls because they lack experience and the confidence to speak up for themselves. They are more willing to do whatever. But, ladies, please be mindful that all that glitters ain't gold. Some of these rappers and athletes and actors may have more than just their star status to offer you. If they don't break your heart, some of them can kill you—literally.

And if you're a parent of a girl, you can be working your fingers to the bone every single day for your child—sending her to private school, saving to buy her a little car for her seventeenth birthday. You can give her diamond studs on her eighteenth birthday and even pay for the full ride to college. And still you can lose your little girl to the lure of some damn rapper.

And for that girl, it isn't the material things that are the lure, it's the bragging rights, it's the special feeling she gets. Do you know what it's like when a man who can have anybody, any girl, looks at you? I do. It's special. At the end of the day you're thinking, "Out of all of the girls in the world, he wants me!" That is special. You could be gorgeous and know it, but to have it confirmed by a platinum artist who is number one on the charts, do you know what that is like? That is sheer heaven even if it's only for one night. "He wanted *me*, I must be hot!"

But consider this: Not how many rappers have herpes or other diseases, but how few don't. Doctors' offices are not private. I get faxes, letters, and actual medical records from doctors all the time. It's disgusting.

I see the groupie thing so much that it has stopped me from wanting the few girlfriends that I have to come out with me when I have to do appearances or when I have extra passes for a party. It's disgusting to me because I consider my girlfriends to be smart women with graduate degrees and good family backgrounds. But put them in the room with a dirty rapper, what?! They love it. Even they turn into chicken heads.

I had one friend who was messing with a rapper. It was just about the sex, but she thought it could be more. As a matter of fact, I had two girlfriends who messed around with rappers, and they both thought it could be more, because the rappers live such hard lives and deal with nothing but chicken heads. Both of my friends thought they would be different—a breath of fresh air from the chicken heads—a cut above the rest. Guess what? They got treated just like the so-called chicken heads—graduate degrees, good-paying jobs, solid family background, and all. They were nothing special to a man who could have anyone.

To women who think they can settle a rapper, I wish you luck! I'm not going to deter you, because I hate blanket statements. Unless you were down with the man from the time he was broke, the way Cookie was down with Magic from the beginning, you have only a slim shot at bagging one of these men for good.

If you meet him when he's on top, he's looking at you like you're a groupie. We don't care to see it that way, but it is what it is. And if you don't believe me, go ahead and try it. Maybe you *are* different. Too often it ends up that he has women in every state and will end up having children outside of your relationship.

And if you're looking for security and he's a rapper, beware. What looks good with the money today is bad the next day. He won't have the money for the child support once he's no longer at the top of the charts. It would end up being a disaster.

Again, that's why I believe women must concentrate on laying *their* foundation. With a good foundation you can weather a storm. You can weather any storm.

DEAR WENDY,

I have a problem that needs to be addressed. During the past few months my six-year-old son, who is in the first grade, came home and told my husband and me that his teacher said that there was no such thing as Santa Claus. This raised a red flag for us, but we didn't care too much because we are not big advocates of Santa Claus anyway.

Then recently, my son lost his two front teeth and even though we were not Tooth Fairy freaks, we put a five-dollar bill under his pillow. Well, imagine my surprise when my son came home saying that his teach told him there is no such thing as the Tooth Fairy and that we were the ones who put the money under the pillow.

But this is not the worst of it. Yesterday, my best friend and I caught the end of the Martin Luther King documentary on PBS. Since I know my son was studying Martin Luther King with the pending holiday, I called him into my bedroom to see the end of the program. Afterward he turned to me and said, "Mommy, you know, Mr. Johnson said that white people killed Martin Luther King." I turned to him and said, "What does a white person look like?" He said, "Like you, Mommy. You're white."

Wendy, I am not white. I'm Cuban and Puerto Rican with green eyes and very light skin and my husband is black. Can you imagine the shit this teacher is feeding him? I need to know what to say to this teacher and to my son. I feel as if this teacher has done a lot of damage to my son and that I have to be very delicate in undoing it. I need to know how to approach this from both angles.

I know you can help me, Wendy. I listen to you every day and I know you will have an intelligent solution to my problem.

APPALLED AND CONFUSED IN BROOKLYN

WENDY'S ADVICE:

This is a woman who shares my sentiments regarding Santa Claus and the Tooth Fairy. I believe you should go along with it and tell your kids the truth sooner or later. But the parents should be the one doing the explaining—not some teacher!

This teacher was way out of bounds. I would have jumped on my broom and flown into that classroom and ripped that teacher a new behind hole. Then I would have gone to the principal and let the principal know that it is unacceptable for the teacher to say the things this teacher said.

Then I would be sure that I was at the next parent-teacher conference or open house, because you know there are other parents there and I would need to find out if this teacher is a killjoy for their children as well.

It is not a teacher's responsibility to kill a child's joy, nor is it the teacher's responsibility to drive home mythical people like Santa and the Tooth Fairy. I don't want them telling my child that there is a Santa or Tooth Fairy either.

I am more concerned about the Martin Luther King matter. Santa and Tooth Fairy are easily explained. I told my son that the Tooth Fairy lived a long time ago and this is what she used to do and we continue the tradition, and Santa Claus lived a long time ago and he spread joy to those less fortunate so we celebrate Santa every December 25.

In terms of Martin Luther King and Mr. Johnson (that's a black name, but is this a black man or a white man?), the best thing that I can suggest is that you get as much material as you can regarding Martin Luther King, including videos and things that a six-year-old can understand, and explain the nonviolence that Dr. King believed in. I would show him why he is able to go to school with black kids and white kids.

I think your son will be fine. Mr. Johnson needs a beat-down but Dr. King said no violence, so don't let your son find out about that beat-down.

DEAR WENDY,

I know you're a busy woman, so I'll speak quickly. Wendy, I'm pregnant and I want to know how I can go about professionally telling my employer that I'm pregnant and how long should I wait to do so? Should I wait until I'm three or four months pregnant or should I wait until I begin to show? How did you inform your boss about your pregnancy? This is my first pregnancy, so I dreadfully need your guidance.

Signed, PREGNANT AND SCARED

WENDY'S ADVICE:

Well, I see that this fax is coming from Washington Mutual, so this person is working at a bank or lending institution—not an industry, like entertainment, where your waistline matters.

I would inform your boss at three and a half months. Doctors always suggest waiting that three-month period because that way you find out if you're having problems with the pregnancy. If you have to take time off work and so on, you will know then. And God forbid if something happens, you don't want to tell everyone earlier and then have to go around and explain things to everyone. Wait until you are officially out of the woods to spread the news.

Do you know what you intend to do once you have the baby? Do you know how much time you're going to take off of work? Will you even be returning to work? What are the stipulations for maternity leave at your job, and how long have you been at the job?

All of these things need to be taken into account, and I know nothing because you haven't included it. But the newer you are at your job, the more nervous you should be as to whether your job will be there when you get off of maternity leave. If you're in entertainment, you really have to plan your pregnancy. You have to plan right after your platinum album has hit the top of the charts. Then you can lay low for nine months and chill and take another three months off, then go into the studio and work on the next album.

And when you're in entertainment you have to worry about whether your waist will snap back fast. Pregnancy weight is cute and motherly for a minute. After that, it becomes pathetic.

DEAR WENDY,

I just found out that my man is bisexual. He said he loves me and doesn't want to leave me. We have been together for six years and I love him dearly. I asked him if he can stop seeing other men and he said he can't. He says he likes men a lot. What do I do? I don't think I can deal with him.

I've had experiences with women, so I can't blame him. But it really bothers me about him. Am I being a hypocrite by not being able to deal with him?

Signed, UNSURE

WENDY'S ADVICE:

A cheater is a cheater! Whether he is cheating with a man or a woman, he's cheating on you and telling you that he is not going to stop. I don't know how old you are, but you have been with him for six years and you don't mention children, so hopefully there are none, which will make your exit a lot easier. Good luck.

You know, gaydar is a wonderful thing. It's not foolproof, but it's a wonderful thing. And there is an overwhelming number of men these days who are involved with women *and* with men.

I'm one of those people who believe man-on-man sex is a totally different ball game from woman-on-woman sex. I think that a lot of women are just experimenting with lesbianism because it's a cool thing to do, and also because men are treating us so badly in a lot of cases that we don't know where else to go. So we just give up, throw in the towel, and turn to women. But that's not the right thing, either, because there is still a problem at hand—our inability to face our problem head-on, without running to something else.

There are, to be sure, women who have no problem being with a bisexual man. And I say, if that's your thing, go for it! But you should know what you're getting into. I don't like surprises, especially surprises like that. And you would be astonished at the number of men living double lives. They are gay and working on Wall Street and know that they will never rise because they don't have the all-important accessories—a wife, kids—so they get a wife and never bother to tell her, "Um, honey, I really like men." Hell, she may be okay with it as long as she gets to live a certain lifestyle. She may go along with the charade. And perhaps it's not a charade as much as a tool of the trade.

While people, in my opinion, take marriage too lightly today, in business being married is important. It separates the men from the boys. And it says that you are stable. I know someone who will not do business with a single man or with a man who is not in a stable relationship. And I understand why. He says if he does do business with a man who is single, he has to allow for the dumbing-out-for-a-woman factor. He has to make provisions for that in the business deal. Isn't that something?

At the end of the day, there are some things that still haven't changed. And that is the picture that marriage presents. It damn sure doesn't mean that it's a true picture. But it's a picture that people want to see.

So I can't hate if, ladies, you meet a man and he's going to be the next Bill Gates and he needs an arm charm, someone to call his missus, someone to have his children and kind of decorate the rest of his life, and he happens to be gay. Go for it. What two consenting adults do is their business. What I don't like is the whole deception. The deception of no protection—making you think you are the only one, marrying you and having kids with you, and *then* you find out that he's gay.

Women write me about the craziest situations. I get this a lot: women who get pissed off at their men and they write me or call me and expect me to put them on blast. I generally do not do this. But I get that all the time. I get it from the girlfriend or boyfriend of a star and I get that from the average Jane Doe. They want to put him on blast!

I tell them, "I'm not putting them on blast. *You* put them on blast!" To me, the best way to put someone who has done you wrong on blast is to move on and be successful. Success is the best revenge. Calling the radio and wanting me to talk about it is very childish. Maybe I need to start putting the blasters on blast.

Here's an example of such a case:

DEAR WENDY,

I'm part of this industry that we speak of so much. I'm six months pregnant with Buddy's baby. Buddy [not his real name] and I have been off and on for a while. A couple of years ago, I was pregnant with his child and I made a decision to have an abortion. When he found out about my decision he was upset and called me selfish. Fast-forward to now, I am six months pregnant and he knows. After regretting my decision some years ago and with him asking me not to have an abortion, this time I decided to keep it.

Now, here comes the hard part. I found out that he has gotten another woman pregnant, and when I confronted him he complained that it wasn't his. Also, I was carrying twins and lost one. During this whole ordeal I have not seen or spoken with Buddy. Rather than him calling me, his wife has been harassing me. Yes, his *wife*! This is the wife he has never claimed and has said was his baby's mother.

This man has not picked up the phone to see how the baby and I are doing. Despite the nasty taste this man has left in my mouth, I don't regret keeping the baby. Right now, I'm awaiting the birth of my son with no regrets, but it is also time to make sure this motherfucker pays. It's time for me to start taking care of things for my baby, even though this man has no real money but is hoping his career gets back on track.

Wendy, I want your advice on what to do, and feel free to say Buddy's name on the air. His people listen all the time and I'm ready to put his ass on blast. Thanks a lot.

—READY TO RUMBLE

WENDY'S ADVICE:

I'm not putting anybody's behind on blast. You got yourself into this situation!

See, women are still under the illusion that getting pregnant and having babies is so easy. But I'm telling you, if you decide to take off the condom you have to think, "What if I become pregnant with twins and I lose one and I have to spend weeks in the hospital and I need him there?" I mean, he hasn't been there and won't be there. He's married. And you're mad because his wife called you? You're the harlot. To you I say: Welcome to the world of single motherhood, and expect more surprises from your baby's father.

And by the way, Buddy is also a straight-up homosexual. Maybe this is something you don't know, but I thought you ought to. This very handsome R & B singer who comes from a Midwest family in the business is a straight-up homosexual.

DEAR WENDY,

I've been engaged for almost a year. I'm twenty-four years old and my fiancé is twenty-nine. While we talk about ideas for our wedding, there are no official plans yet. The problem is that while I love my man dearly, I'm no longer sure I want to marry him.

We were together for two years before he proposed. He is truly my best friend. We share a lot of the same values and want some of the same things in life. However, he is stuck on this 1950s housewife role for me.

While I believe I'm competent to be a wife and mother and a career woman, he believes my role should be to cook and clean and be a wife. He makes enough money to run our household and he has made it clear that it is my choice if I want to work. However, I don't want to sit home and do nothing.

Yes, Wendy, I cook dinner every night. But I also work every day. The reason for my second thoughts about marriage is that even though I want as many children as God will bless me with, I believe my man will insist that I be a stay-at-home mom. I think he's being unreasonable. What do you think?

—MODERN-DAY WOMAN

WENDY'S ADVICE:

I think that the writing is on the wall. You understand what you're dealing with and you communicated it very effectively to me. This is not the man for you. And if you marry him, he is going to remind you time and time again while you fight, what a woman's role is and what a man's role is. He will say, "I told you this before we got married, so why are you acting like it's new, now?" This is not the man for you. You are twenty-four and you have plenty of time. Keep it moving.

My first husband was into those traditional roles. I rather liked it because, ideally, I believe in traditional roles. I come from traditional roles. I know it sounds corny, but I know nothing else. I watched my mother work and my mother cook. Every day at five o'clock dinner was on the table. She was a great cook, a fabulous cook. She decorated and entertained with ease. She and my father would pick us up at our various extracurricular activities. But at the end of the day, my mother was the one in the laundry room folding the clothes. And she was the one soaking the ham to get the salt out of it to make Sunday dinner. And she was the one waking up at six in the morning trying to get us to the school and then get herself to school, because she was a teacher. So I don't know anything but traditional roles. And I like it.

But there are a lot of things about being a woman these days that aren't traditional. And those are the things that my ex-husband had a problem with. Like a women making more money than a man. Like a woman working hours that aren't nine to five. Many of us have to work after hours. In my profession, going out to various social functions that involve me having to work after hours is the norm. My job also involves me working after hours with fewer clothes on than if I were an attorney doing so. The clothes are tighter, the clothes are skimpier. I'm having drinks, so there's this illusion that I'm having this great grandiose time. And my ex-husband couldn't deal with it.

So when I was faced with the decision of whether to work it

out or bail, I decided to bail, because we had no children and there wasn't a lot invested in the relationship yet. I was only married for five months when we had a huge, explosive fight over these very issues. And that was the end. I called up my parents and made the announcement and I called up my attorney and I started getting everything in line.

Now, I'm happily married. And I've been married now for almost six years and the roles are still traditional. It's just that my husband is with me on the after-hours hustle. Hell, he's the one who arranges for it to go down. My husband is my manager and he has a perfect, clear understanding of what I want out of life, in terms of my career. As long as I have the drive to do it, he is there to support me. But at the end of the day, it's still my responsibility to pick out the carpet and make sure that it gets laid. I love decorating the house, and he leaves me to do it, just like the woman from the 1950s, and I love that. It's my responsibility to rustle up some form of dinner or make a formal announcement that there is no dinner and that we're going out to eat. And it's my job to find a good pediatrician for our son and get him registered for school and all that.

And it becomes very challenging. There are many days that I show up for my radio show and I tell you people that I am so happy to talk with you, and I truly mean that. You help me take my mind off the stress of my life. You help me take my mind off of my troubles the way you tell me that I help take your mind off of your troubles.

Not that my life is so terrible, but I'm just saying that the roles that my husband and I have are very much like those of the fifties. I don't go out for girls' night out, but then again we discussed this on our first date. We established this early in our relationship. I was never the girls'-night-out kind. And he didn't want a woman who wanted a girls' night out. When he gets stressed he wants to go out and drink some Hennessy with his boys. I'm the type of woman who will stay in the house and wish him well. "Have fun, honey! I'll be here when you get back."

Vacationing apart is fine for some marriages, and it's fine for some women and fine for some men. That's not how we get down. But you have to communicate these preferences very early in your relationship—before it turns to love and marriage and baby carriage. You have to establish your likes and dislikes, because I'll tell you this, people do not change.

If a guy tells you from the jump that he doesn't like makeup and weaves, he's not going to all of a sudden start liking makeup and weaves because you're his wife. A guy who tells you he wants you to cook and clean is not going to change his mind because you're his wife.

How we handle it at my house is I don't cook and I don't clean, but I do know how to make a little money. So therefore, I have to line up the help. I make it work. I may not do the cooking and the cleaning, but I make it happen and I get it done.

I love makeup and I love plastic surgery and I love fake hair and my husband knew that on our first date. There were no surprises. And it's the same today.

DEAR WENDY,

I need some advice. Me and one of my homegirls have been friends for seven years. We are really close and we speak every day on the phone. We hang out together, whether it's shopping or going out to eat or going to the club. Everyone knows to look for us together, because we usually are. Now the issue is, I met her through my brother; she was my brother's girlfriend for about five of the seven years that I have known her. My brother lives in Atlanta and has now moved on and so has she. But he is furious that we are still friends.

Apparently when they stopped dealing, we were supposed to stop being friends. But we have developed a relationship of our own. We don't talk or make references to my brother. In fact, his name hardly comes up. We just have a lot of the same interests and like to do a lot of the same things. And now over the years I can honestly say that she has been a friend to me, and in return I have been a friend to her, as if we had never met through my brother. So now, two years after their breakup, when I do speak to my brother he has smart comments and will only refer to her in a sarcastic way like she is the only friend I have and I worship her or something, which is totally ridiculous. Now my friend feels bad, because she doesn't want to come between me and my brother.

He doesn't even live here, Wendy! My question to you is, I don't live in Atlanta anymore so I don't care. And what's crazy is that my brother and my friend still speak maybe once every two weeks. What do I do? Stop hanging out and being friends to spare my brother's feelings? Or do we tell him to grow up and ac-knowledge that we are friends?

—Do I lose my friend?

Wendy's Advice:

Well, it sounds like a wonderful relationship you have with this woman. And you're in so deep. How close are you with your brother? This is a really tough one. I'm going to leave it up to you.

But I can make a statement to other men and women who

come up with this problem in the future. When your sibling says it's over, it's over. All ties get cut. I'm just giving it to you from my side.

My brother, Tommy, is the only brother that I have, and we talk maybe four times a week. He lives about twenty minutes away from me in New Jersey, and he's married. But if he wasn't and he was dating, I wouldn't be friendly with his girlfriends like that. I would be as friendly as he wants me to be. And if he breaks up with them, it's over. I don't know you anymore, girl! It was nice to know you, but that's my brother and it's over!

I roll with my siblings. I'm sorry, I don't care if they're dating or married. I roll with what they want me to roll with, because I have a very cool sister and a very cool brother and there is nobody outside of them that would matter more. And I'm sure they would do the same thing. They love my husband to death, but they roll with me and that's the way it is. My lines of loyalty are real simple.

The thing about advice is that no one has all of the answers (especially not me). Not even our parents had all the answers, and their parents didn't have all the answers.

I wish that I had known that my parents didn't have all the answers when I was growing up, because maybe I wouldn't have had to deal with so many issues—issues that I am still dealing with. A lot of them I have overcome, but for those of you who listen to my radio show, you might question where some of my honesty comes from. It comes from not wanting to present this perfect picture. Because that's not real.

A woman who's married with a career does not have a perfect life. I wish that more people in influential positions could be honest. People have body issues; God knows I have mine. People lie about fidelity in their marriage. People lie about how great their kids are and how wonderful their life is. People lie about how much they love sex. People lie because they want to fit in, because they believe everyone else has a perfect life and they don't want to seem different.

When the truth is, we are all trying to figure our way through life. And it takes the pressure off of people if they know that somebody is willing to admit, "I don't have all the answers, and I'm not perfect."

Being sought out for advice is extremely flattering. But it also creates a lot of pressure, because I don't have all of the answers. There are some questions that are easy to answer—as easy as telling people to call a private eye, an attorney, or a doctor. But there are more challenging questions. And some of the questions make me really scared.

I will look at the fax and it's signed by a schoolteacher. And I'm thinking, "Oh, my God! This is a person teaching our kids." Or I will get an off-the-wall fax from a person with a master's or a Ph.D. and I'm thinking, "Is this what graduate school is producing?"

I get scared for all of us, because you people are coming to me for advice and I don't have all the answers. And I'm perfectly honest and okay with saying I don't. But if I can help you find some answers for yourself, I guess it's worth it.

About the Authors

Wendy Williams's previous book, *Wendy's Got the Heat,* was a *New York Times* best seller. Her radio program, *The Wendy Williams Experience,* airs nationally and on WBLS 107.5 in New York City. Wendy Williams live in New Jersey with her husband and their son.

Karen Hunter has collaborated on the best sellers *Wendy's Got the Heat, I Make My Own Rules* with LL Cool J, *Ladies First* with Queen Latifah, and *On the Down Low* with JL King.